You Can Go Home Again

American University Studies

Series XXIV
American Literature
Vol. 45

PETER LANG
New York • San Francisco • Bern • Baltimore
Frankfurt am Main • Berlin • Wien • Paris

Rebecca Luttrell Briley

You Can Go Home Again

The Focus on Family in the Works of Horton Foote

PETER LANG
New York • San Francisco • Bern • Baltimore
Frankfurt am Main • Berlin • Wien • Paris

Library of Congress Cataloging-in-Publication Data

Briley, Rebecca Luttrell.
    You can go home again : the focus on family in the works of Horton Foote / Rebecca Luttrell Briley.
       p.   cm. — (American university studies. Series XXIV, American literature ; vol. 45)
    Includes bibliographical references.
    1. Foote, Horton—Criticism and interpretation.   2. Domestic drama—History and criticism.   3. Family in literature.   I. Title. II. Series.
PS3511.0344Z59   1993   812'.54—dc20   92-45641
ISBN 0-8204-2004-2   CIP
ISSN 0895-0512

Die Deutsche Bibliothek-CIP-Einheitsaufnahme

Briley, Rebecca Luttrell:
You can go home again : the focus on family in the works of Horton Foote / Rebecca Luttrell Briley.–New York ; Berlin ; Bern ; Frankfurt/M. ; Paris ; Wien : Lang, 1993
   (American university studies : Ser. 24, American literature ; Vol. 45)
   ISBN 0-8204-2004-2
NE: American university studies/24

The paper in this book meets the guidelines for permanence and durability of the Committee on Production Guidelines for Book Longevity of the Council on Library Resources.

© Peter Lang Publishing, Inc., New York 1993

All rights reserved.
Reprint or reproduction, even partially, in all forms such as microfilm, xerography, microfiche, microcard, offset strictly prohibited.

Printed in the United States of America.

Table of Contents

1 Horton Foote: An Introduction 1

2 "Always Doing Texas": The Early Plays 19

3 Adapting for a Living: 49
    Part I: Foote-prints in Faulkner Films: Adaptations of "Old Man," "Tomorrow," and "Barn Burning" 49
    Part II: Climbing into Another Writer's Skin: Adapting *To Kill a Mockingbird* 62
    Part III: "Getting into the Nature of Adapting": Other Adaptations for Hollywood and Television 77

4 "A Voice of His Own": The Original Screenplays 89
    Part I: "The Traveling Lady" and *Baby the Rain Must Fall* 89
    Part II: *The Chase*: Three Genres in One 97
    Part III: The *Tender Mercies* of Independent Film Making 106
    Part IV: The Successful *Trip[s] to Bountiful* 116

5 The Final Homecoming: *The Orphans' Home* Cycle 129

6 The Later One-Acts: A Darker Vision 163

7 The Final Assessment 189

Works Cited 199

Dedication

for Kyle, in loving memory and gratitude,
and
for Lillian Vallish Foote,
both of whom died in 1992 after this study was completed.

Chapter One

Horton Foote: An Introduction

According to New York *Times* critic Samuel G. Freedman, playwright and screenwriter Horton Foote has "for too long remained a relative secret in American literature" (xii). For although most people recognize the three Oscar-winning films for which he wrote screenplays: *To Kill a Mockingbird, Tender Mercies,* and *The Trip to Bountiful,* few recall the writer's name. Just the aforementioned trio of works warrants paying attention to this retiring and gentle elderly man who, at seventy-four, shows little sign of actually retiring from his profession; however, examination of his canon reveals a prolific career studded with less prominent, but no less promising, literature for both audience and scholar alike.

Tracing a prevalent theme of homecoming and reconciliation between fathers and their children throughout the works, this study will attempt to scrutinize all available material from this little-known 20th century American dramatist. Foote has demonstrated his interest in the family and its role in society by focusing on the relationships between parents and their children in most, if not all, of his writing career. He displays particular insight into the union between fathers and their sons and examines the importance the influence a strong, loving father has in the development of the child. His use of personal regional material differentiates his plays from other American drama, but that alone does not set Foote's work apart from other modern writers. That his entire canon highlights a single theme of the family, especially the relationship between fathers and sons, is significant and demands attention, but other writers have maintained a single theme throughout their work, as well.

What does distinguish Foote from his contemporaries, however, is the demonstrated determination to concentrate on the development of character over the other elements of play writing and his compassionate approach to characterization. Almost without exception, Foote depicts his characters as human beings, complete with flaws and virtues alike, providing insight into their misdirected lives to elicit the sympathy of his audience. This adherence to realism in his work has led Foote to develop beyond his initial optimistic view of life; examination of the entire canon reveals a progressive darkening of Foote's perspective on society.

However, in spite of this more somber tone to Foote's later work, rarely does Foote indicate a loss of hope. Most of his plays, having illustrated a realistic picture of a fragmented modern American society, culminate in the promise of reconciliation for all characters who are willing to change and to reestablish relationships with family members. Throughout his work, the playwright extends his definition of family from the individual to the larger community, as well, demonstrating the universality of his theme. His charity toward characters and his unshaken belief in the possibility of hopeful family reunion does separate Foote's work from the bulk of most modern writing, American or otherwise; and the readiness with which much of Foote's work lends itself to spiritual interpretation, as defined by the Southern protestantism from which Foote writes, places it in a class by itself. Finally, his creation of the nine-play cycle, *The Orphans' Home*, is a unique contribution to American drama; no other playwright has created a cycle of equal length, maintaining at the same time a single theme. It is the purpose of this study to illuminate the above in the works of Horton Foote.

While little has been published concerning Horton Foote, other than film and stage reviews, there are students who appreciate Foote and his work, either for its subject matter or for the contributions he has made to the American stage and screen. Foremost among these is Gerald Wood, who has published Foote's selected one-act plays, introducing each with his own commentary; Wood is currently compiling material for Foote's authorized biography.[1] Interviews conducted between

Wood and Foote that reveal significant insights into the writer's life and work also have been made available in print.

Terry Barr has completed the only other dissertation on Foote and his work,[2] focusing on this broad thesis: Foote's characters as "ordinary people." Filling out his study are brief remarks on Foote's relationship with a few of the major playwrights of the 1930's-1950's and a thorough examination of the role Foote played in American television in the late 1940's and 1950's. The latter emphasis makes Barr's 1986 work valuable; three lengthy personal interviews with Horton Foote add interesting detail.

Most other articles are of a personal or more biographical nature, introducing the little-known writer to an audience growing in size and appreciation; many of these short publications repeat the same facts and stories. Gary Edgerton has written a piece for *Literature/Film Quarterly* that carefully traces Foote's film career and examines the impact Foote's approach has had on Hollywood and independent film making.[3]

A glance at the roots of Foote's development as a writer reveals the literary profession was not his first choice. Initially, Foote left his home in Wharton, Texas, in 1933, at the age of 17 "to pursue a call to become an actor," first in California and then in New York City where he became involved with the American Actors Theatre (AAT). In an interview, he explains, "I had no intention of being a writer. . . . I never in my wildest dreams ever thought I'd ever be a writer" (Edgerton 3). As the AAT was in need of scripts, however, Foote, along with a few others in the group, began to experiment with play writing. Under the leadership of director Mary Hunter, who believed Broadway was devoid of any "real knowledge of American life," the AAT took as its "primary intention . . . the uncovering of our own cultural roots" (Hunter 5).

As the members of the troupe came from different parts of the United States, it was decided that exploring these represented areas through script writing would be interesting for the company, as well as enlightening to the American public. "In preparing all these works," Foote recalls, "we would improvise . . . someone from Minnesota would do an improvisation from Minnesota, so we would get to know what that region was like, and I was always doing Texas" (Edgerton 4).

"Always doing Texas," Foote not only introduced the company to "what that region was like," but also began to develop within himself what would become the constant setting and background of his work. He elaborates, "I got in touch with material that was . . . for lack of a better word, regional material. . . . I really believe this material chose me more than I chose it." The major theme of his plays also began to formulate during these early years. He goes on to explain, "I've been told and I really agree, that by the time one is ten years old, at least for a certain brand of writer who writes like I write, that their themes have been set. You can take them out and put them in different periods at different times . . . but it is amazing to me how many of these themes keep repeating themselves, or attitudes, or approaches to character" (Edgerton 4).

At another time, Foote commented: "Themes are given to us at a very early age. We spend our life instinctively searching to reinforce those themes. Our writing style is within us. I wonder if we can't change our themes or style any more than we can the color of our eyes or skin" (Personal communication 11/13/87). One of these recurring themes to which Foote alludes is that of the importance of families and the relationships between fathers and their children on which this study will focus. Since the influence of his own family background on his life and writing has been greater than any other force in his life, Foote has "spent his life" reinforcing that theme in his work. He sees his vision as universal, however, and objects to the term "regional" (Personal communication 11/14/87). Despite the fact that most of his material stems from his personal background, Foote sees the message of his work as applicable everywhere.

When Foote later added writing for television to his play writing profession, he found a kindred spirit in Fred Coe, the NBC producer for whom Foote wrote most of his teleplays. Foote credits Coe with encouraging him to explore his own material. "He didn't want us to copy and try to find formulas," Foote remembers. "He used to say who are you as a writer, and what can you write that no one else can write?" Foote considers Coe's advice to avoid "formulas that would please many people" in favor of "deeply pleas[ing] ourselves" to be the greatest lesson anyone in the profession ever gave him (Edgerton 5). Even though many directors and producers would disagree along the way with this personal approach to script writing, and its popularity would rise and fall throughout Foote's career, he nurtured Coe's advice, aware of the truth it held for him as a writer.

Foote's reputation in the 1940's grew as he was praised by New York critics as one of the "promising playwrights" (Barr 40). Soon his talents were sought out by Hollywood producers and directors who discouraged this use of "regional" and personal material in favor of more commercially lucrative themes and sophisticated approaches. Director Howard Lindsay went so far as to advise Foote to "write about people you wouldn't invite into your livingroom" (41). In his quiet but stubborn way, Foote stood by his own instincts, even when that decision momentarily interfered with his professional progress. He defends his position when he explains:

> From the beginning most of my plays have taken place in the imaginary town of Harrison, Texas, and it seems to me a more unlikely subject could not be found in these days of Broadway and world theatre, than this attempt of mine to recreate a small southern town and its people. But I did not choose this task, this place, or these people to write about so much as they chose me, and I try to write of them with honesty (Locher 210).

Foote was equally protective of his style from those "days of Broadway and world theatre." Barr points out that the two more prominent "strains" in the American theatre of the 1930's and 1940's, political and sentimental, influenced Foote's work only in the sense that like those writers, his work also concentrated on "the lives and dilemmas of the ordinary American" (16). Foote has never consciously been a political playwright like many of his contemporaries of the theatre in the 1930's, especially those members of The Group Theatre; for example, Foote admits he did not care for Clifford Odets' *Waiting for Lefty*, as "it was too overtly political" (17). In an interview with Freedman, Foote explains:

> I have social points of view that are not shared by a lot of people, but I never picked fights much. I listened to them and tried to understand what made them feel the way they did. Not that I've ever understood, but I've learned to listen. I'm a social writer in the sense that I want to record, but not in the sense of trying to change people's minds (xix).

Neither was he drawn to the experimental forms of expressionistic theatre so striking in American drama in the 1920's and 1930's; other than occasional similarities in subject matter, Foote's style bears little resemblance to that of Eugene O'Neill, Elmer Rice, or Thornton Wilder. Roger Fristoe, of the Louisville *Courier-Journal*, has labeled Foote "the benign Eugene O'Neill" (SBTS), but only because much of his work is autobiographical, as was O'Neill's in part, and not for the use of symbolism and expressionistic stagecraft associated with O'Neill's contribution to the stage. Foote claims that when he saw O'Neill's work for the first time, he "experienced no emotional involvement" (Personal communication 11/13/87), the ultimate test of a play by Foote's standard; O'Neill's attempts to establish new theatrical styles did not impress him.

Just as Foote cannot be associated with the political movement in play writing of this time, neither can he be connected to its tendency toward sentimentalism, the other "strain" Barr mentions. Only rarely is there evidence of the sentimental optimism found in other contemporaries of that period, such as William Saroyan, or the witticism and humor in the popular theatre of writers like George Kaufman and Moss Hart or Ben Hecht and Charles MacArthur. That is not to say, of course, that Foote's work lacks optimism or humor (further discussion will suggest the contrary); but, Foote has refused repeatedly "to compromise his themes and characters with consistently unrealistic, happy endings" (Barr 20). This commitment to realism becomes particularly apparent in the later work, as Foote's vision of society seems to have darkened progressively.

Though Foote was interested in what he calls "dance theatre" and wrote several pieces for modern dance interpretation, his work is unrelated to the musical; the ever-present use of music in his plays is for underscoring a theme, rather than entertaining or dazzling an audience. Foote did work alongside Paul Green and Lynn Riggs in his early days in New

York, but it is their focus on regional material that creates a viable comparison with Foote and not their association with the musical.

Comparisons could be drawn between an isolated work or two of Maxwell Anderson, but Anderson's fascination with both historical and verse plays cut short any easy connections that may be suggested between him and Foote. Foote uses the historical chiefly for personal reasons to record a time past, and his dialogue, unlike Anderson's self-conscious poetizing, is authentic to his Texan characters and does not even suggest poetry. Except for a few early plays, Foote has shown a tendency to withdraw from the "well-made" play form. For this reason, and his conscious attempt to avoid the melodramatic, little can be said concerning his relationship to the works of other such prominent American writers of this period as Sidney Howard, Robert Sherwood, or Lillian Hellman. In fact, Foote's distaste for Hellman's tendency toward the melodramatic manifested itself during a joint film project to be discussed later.

With the playwrights of the late 1940's and 1950's and their focus on realistic "kitchen-sink" drama and its partiality for character over plot, Foote appears to be more at home. Superficial readings of such writers as Robert Anderson and William Inge invite comparison, as these authors, like Foote, often write of the daily grind of small-town America. However, Foote's interest in the intimate portrayal of character through dialogue, rather than in plot and social commentary, sets his work apart from these American writers. He does not share the tendency toward pessimism, either, of writers like Inge, as Foote's plays tend to offer hope, in spite of realistic, even depressing, situations.

That is not to say that Foote rightfully shares a position of greatness with the two more important writers of this period, Arthur Miller and Tennessee Williams. His inconsistent creation of memorable characters in unique experiences that appeal to a broad audience restricts Foote's work from achieving standards set by the giants of modern drama. Foote, however, is the first to dismiss any connections between himself and these two more prominent leaders of American theatre.

Claiming he does not "share the same aesthetic" with Arthur Miller, Foote sees little in Miller's work to admire or emulate. Disdaining the "common man" Miller champions in favor of the "uncommon man," Foote insists he is "too interested in the particulars" to be drawn to Miller's subjects (Wood, *LFQ* 233). Closer inspection, however, of a dominant theme in Miller's work of fathers and sons and their expectations and disappointments in each other, as seen in such significant works as *All My Sons*, *The Death of a Salesman*, and *After the Fall*, suggests a relationship Foote may have overlooked. However, it is significant that although both writers seem to focus on the importance of the father-son union, while Miller's work has a consistent tendency toward pessimism, Foote's maintains an equally consistent tendency toward hope. The comparison between Foote and Miller is illustrative of what distinguishes Foote's work from most modern writing.

Sharing his Southern roots with Tennessee Williams, with whom he was friends in the early days of their careers, suggests further connections between these two playwrights; Foote was even given the opportunity to direct "The Gentleman Caller" scene in Williams' initial production of *The Glass Menagerie*. Foote admits, however, that this play is the only one of Williams' that he appreciates; "I admire him," he confided in an interview with Wood, "but I don't like him. . . . I feel the others [plays following *The Glass Menagerie*] were a little overwrought for my taste" (Wood, *LFQ* 226).

Foote's "taste" is one of understatement. A student of the "less is more" principle, Foote claims there is too much "real drama" for fiction, meaning that incidents from life do not need embellishment to create interesting theatre. "Pull back, pull back, and get away from it," he advises (Wood, *LFQ* 235). So while F. Scott Fitzgerald once wrote that "action is character," where Foote's style is concerned, it would be more appropriate to say "character is action." It is this emphasis in his work that links him more with Chekhov than with any other playwright. As illustrated particularly in *The Three Sisters* and *The Cherry Orchard*, Chekhov's on-stage focus is on character and its on-stage reaction to off-stage action. For this reason especially, actor Robert Duvall, long-time friend and participant in Foote work, calls Foote's style "rural Chekhov—simple but deep" (*CBY* 146).

The glaring gap between the avant-garde playwrights of the 1960's and Horton Foote speaks for itself. It is absurd even to mention the Theatre of the Absurd, La Mama, the Living Theatre, or The San Francisco Mime Troupe, for example, in the same breath with Horton Foote. Nor can any connection be drawn with Jack Gelber or Julian Beck, Lee Breuer or Megan Terry, or any of the other leaders of the experimental, agit-prop movement of that decade; and while some thematic similarities on the crisis in the modern American family may surface when discussing Edward Albee, the comparison falters beyond that. Albee does not concern himself with the hope for societal rehabilitation that Foote's work maintains.

The same could be said for the forerunners of the theatre of the 1970's and 1980's: Kopit, McNally, Guare, or Rabe, to mention a few, and the more significant Sam Shepard and David Mamet. Again, comparisons in subject matter with the occasional romantic Shepard script could be drawn, but the differences between the two writers far outweigh their similarities. With Lanford Wilson, who also often writes of small-town America, Foote shares his preference for character development over plot, but, once again, a difference in philosophy limits the comparison. Foote acknowledges the obvious disparities between himself and the Shepards and Mamets of current play writing, but refuses to criticize or offer much opinion on the direction of modern drama.

Unwilling to ignore those who have carved an individual niche for themselves in modern theatre, Foote has said, however, that while he, Shepard, and Mamet have different points of view, "we admire each other"; he cites Shepard's "toaster scene" from *True West* as evidence of Shepard's "good sense of physical action." Although he feels that Mamet may have a tendency to "do anything to be successful," he openly respects Mamet's "vital force," and praises his colleague for successfully "taking on Hollywood." Foote does credit the 1960's with "one good thing": the revolutionary freedom of the decade that made it possible for the Shepards and the Mamets to "start their own theatres" in order to get their plays produced. "The core is to be respected," Foote adds, "and these [Shepard and Mamet, for example] have made a theatre for themselves" (Personal communication 11/14/87).

"Making a theatre for oneself" may be a goal that Foote shares with his contemporaries, though his theatre would not resemble theirs, of course. Holding fast to what he believes in, Foote calmly insists that the realistic play, with its focus on character, will make a comeback; he even predicts that in ten years "realistic plays will be avant-garde" (Personal communication 11/14/87). Foote has never been more active or sought after in his life than he is now, and if the current increasing popularity of Foote's work is any indication, he may be a prophet.

Whenever Foote has disagreed with a producer or director who does not share his vision for a film, he has withdrawn from the project, erasing his name from the credits. The same can be said of his reaction to the shift to horror and hopelessness in much of 1960's film and theatre when Foote retreated from his profession to work on a personal project based on family stories (the nine-play cycle *The Orphans' Home*), realizing he had nothing in common with what was expected from current writers in either content or form. Offended by the explicit sexual content of modern film and television, too, Foote confesses, "I don't understand the new confessional style of writing. One should have the good taste to disguise it. 'Kiss and tell' is very unpleasant." Then, referring to the current Hollywood penchant for "slash and gash" films, he quips, "Oedipus blinded himself, but he didn't do it on stage" (Personal communication 11/13/87).

Uninterested in, even horrified by what he saw as the rebellious tendency to repel or shock the 1960-1970's audience toward social change, Foote may appear to have hidden his head in the sand of the past as he excused himself from the present scene to retreat into his memories. It was here, however, that Foote reconfirmed for himself his source of truth and hope for survival in this world through connections with one's family, past and present. In the re-creating of those old ways and personages, perhaps an answer could be offered to the angry questions being hurled at a once too-complacent audience. As Freedman put it a couple of years ago, "at the age of seventy-two, [Foote] is a man reborn" (xv).

Armed with a revitalized vision as the "fads" in play writing and film making of the 1960's and 1970's began to fade, Foote reemerged from his seclusion, ready to stage or film the product of his semi-retirement, even if it meant producing his work independently. Although aware that his work could not ignore the degradation of society, perhaps his depiction of what he saw as the source of its degeneration — the erosion of the family nucleus and the exchange of moral values for materialistic greed — could call home any weary prodigals straining to hear an invitation to return. By focusing on the family, perhaps the cure for society's ills would become more discernable.

Apparently, Foote's attempt to offer personal portraits with universal meanings has been successful, for one reviewer, Marian Burkhart for *Commonweal* admits, "I realized that Horton Foote is quite probably America's greatest playwright" when, after seeing a couple of the plays from *The Orphans' Home* cycle, she felt more at home with his characters than with real-life society's present mayhem. "For even if Foote's plays are based upon events in the life of his own family," she explains, "his work turns outward to a world Americans know, an unexaggerated, uninflated world where most of us live" (110). The clarion call Foote's plays emit to an American audience to come home to its roots reverberates throughout Foote's canon, encircling his entire career just as Cynthia Clawson's crooning "Come home, come home, ye who are weary come home" at the opening and closing of his *Trip to Bountiful* ties together that film.

This return to the roots of one's family branches out into several directions in Foote's work. First, the material takes Foote himself back to his heritage, as most of his subject matter is taken from stories he collected while growing up in Wharton, Texas. Second, the characters themselves experience various homecomings, becoming reconciled to their families, particularly their fathers. Third, Foote's "homespun" style takes both Broadway and Hollywood back to a more realistic form, away from what Foote sees as a current absorption with spectacle and action, gore and glitz. And fourth, the audience itself is brought back to a picture album of an America that may have disappeared with Viet Nam and Rambo movies.

This general focus on homecoming defines itself more specifically in Foote's continual dramatic scrutiny of the relationships between parents and their children, usually fathers and sons. This theme is so significant in Foote's work that nearly every single piece, from early one-acts to full-length feature films, revolves around it. On one level, this is a general observation of the roles parents play in their families' lives; as Foote examines the shortcomings in his individual characters, more often than not, on another level, the root of the problem lies in a misconducted parental role. Erik Barnouw, television historian, affirms that Foote's work, along with many others writing for television in the early years, was "forever suggesting that a problem might stem from childhood and be involved with feelings toward a mother or father" (33). Foote concurs, stating in the published notes of his play *Flight*, that "my characters are often searching for a town or a home to belong to, or a parent, or a child—all parts of the family" (149).

In part, Foote's fascination with this topic stems from his sole desire as a writer to be the "recorder" of the family's history, both personal and universal. He considers secondary any role other than that of family scribe (Personal communication 11/14/87). Because he cherishes the history of his family's past and the impact family had on his growing up, he has dedicated his life to collecting the family stories and saving the memory of his people for posterity. But, as he is interested also in the universal and believes that "family" has had similar importance to most of his audience, Foote also extends his definition of "family" to include the community, and the scope of his family's lifetime is expanded to cover that of the community. "These are important people," Foote implies, "and not just to me on the personal level, but for all America. They represent our heritage, our roots, and their way of life is worthy of preservation. From them, perhaps, we can rediscover how to live today."

Like Thomas Wolfe's Eugene Gant, Foote feels the tug of that past on his pant leg that attempts to impede any progress too far from the past. But unlike Wolfe, Foote has proved that one *can* go home again: he has been doing it all his life, both literally and literally, as his homecomings are the source of progress in his life. Born March 14, 1916, to Albert Horton Foote, Sr., the owner of a small clothing store in Wharton, Texas, and the aristocratic Hallie (Brooks) Foote, an accomplished pianist, Albert Horton Foote, Jr., has been returning to Wharton (renamed Harrison in most of his work) and the stories of his family that he says "have haunted me all my life." He calls the result "personal plays" (CBY 143-144), though he objects to the term "autobiographical," insisting he is "far more interested in other people's lives than his own" (Hachem 39).

Ever since he left home as a teenager to begin his career in theatre, Foote did not allow more than two years to elapse without coming home for a visit; he received a daily letter from his mother until she died in 1974 (Freedman xix). Now, although he lives with Lillian, his wife of some forty years, in New Hampshire and Greenwich Village, Foote makes at least five trips home yearly. He bought the family estate a few years ago, along with the last plots in the family cemetery that he used to visit every day while growing up in the small Southern town (Calio 73).

These sojourns in the graveyard have become a local joke that Foote does not mind sharing: "When I came back for a visit two years ago," he told Freedman, "someone said,'Let's throw a party for Horton.' And someone else said,'Where, in the graveyard?'" (Freedman xi) Foote claims this teasing is because, at his age, most of his friends and family are dead. It is just as likely, though, that his townsmen were referring to the love Foote simply has for graveyards. "I love these old tombstones," Foote admits. "I always felt at home here" (xi). His affection for the cemetery and what it represents is evident in his writing: he has made the family graveyard the most important recurring symbol in his plays, and he utilizes visits to the graveyard, along with the necessity of erecting tombstones for loved ones, as an illustration of the significance of maintaining relationships with family members.

Foote's own relationship with his father was not as perfect as one might imagine. Seeing little of his hard-working, stern father during his childhood, Foote now examines many situations in his plays that stem from absent fathers or from mothers who shoulder both parental roles. Daughter Hallie Foote, who agrees that the "father-child relationship manifests itself very strongly in much of [her father's] work," suggests that "in some ways my own father felt my grandfather difficult and fearful and at times somewhat rigid," but she hastens to add that Foote "also had great compassion for him because he understood where all of that came from" (Personal letter 9/5/89).

Foote confesses a closer tie to his mother, but his understanding of his father grew, especially after spending more time with the man by working in the family store as a teenager. It was during these times spent together talking that Foote developed a deeper appreciation for his father. As his half-orphaned father described to Foote his struggle to rear himself without a father, the importance of a good father-son relationship also crystallized in Foote's mind (Barr 9). Although these stories find their ways subtly into most of Foote's writing, *The Orphans' Home*, the nine-play cycle that details the lives of Foote's parents and grandparents, is the fruition of all the talk of the past and the culmination of a loving relationship between Foote and his own father.

Apparently, Foote practices what he learned from his parents and what he has preached in his writing. His eldest daughter, the actress Hallie, confirms that her "relationship to both my mother and father always has been close. I respect them for what they have taught me and for who they are as people." She concludes, "One thing I never doubted was the fact that they both loved me very much and they always made sure I knew that," even when she insisted on her own independence (Personal letter 9/5/89).

For a child to know that it is loved by its parents and that it can rest in the security of their care regardless of the circumstances of its life is the ideal family setting Foote suggests. The thin line a parent walks in providing compassionate discipline rather than unnecessary cruelty in training a child is a constant labor for the parent and often the source of confusion in a young child. Foote, having experienced this dichotomy in his own upbringing, portrays this situation empathetically in his writing; but as he himself came to appreciate the authoritative position his father had to maintain, many of his characters come to develop an understanding for such father-figures in their lives, personal or communial.

This portrayal of authority figures has led many reviewers and readers alike to question the relationship between Foote's characters and God, their "heavenly Father." In some cases, characters are unreconciled to their earthly fathers and remain unreconciled with God; many seek reconciliation with God because their relationships with their own fathers have failed for some reason. But for all these characters, Foote offers the ultimate hope: reconciliation is possible and available for all who seek it, not only with earthly fathers, but also with God, who is not so much an unloving judge as an exacting, perfect Father. Just as Foote's plays suggest that society's ills may stem from broken families, they encourage a spiritual interpretation, intimating that the family's problems may stem from a broken relationship with the "heavenly Father."

Foote will be the first to deny that he is primarily a religious writer, even though he confesses to being a "deeply religious" man. Claiming he does not consciously emphasize religious themes in his work, he goes on to explain that he avoids religious discussions because "it would never occur to me to proselytize" (Wood, *LFQ* 231). He prefers to keep his focus on the earthly family, calling his prodigal characters home to flesh and blood connections. Suggesting that Foote's philosophy is a type of "sacred-humanism," Marian Burkhart writes, "If one recognizes that religion is a matter not of answers but of awe, one can see in what way Foote is religious. Foote ... is in awe before the mystery of human goodness" (113).

However, when pressed to explain the spiritual implications in his work that are obvious to many of his audience, Foote has admitted that religion "must be more deeply rooted in my makeup than I realize" (Wood, *LFQ* 231). Further, Foote has agreed that the father-son relationships in his writing may as easily be interpreted from a spiritual as a human perspective (Personal communication 7/28/89). For the sake of clarity in this study, the term "spiritual" is taken from the Southern protestant milieu in which Foote himself was reared and in which he places his characters.

How people survive in the face of everyday calamity is a theme of Foote's work unearthed by many critics. Foote acknowledges religion is one source of sustaining power for these people with whom he grew up and who find themselves as characters in his plays. "I think there is a lot of strength in the Southern protestant religion. . . . [I have an] abiding deep respect for it, and it is foolish not to recognize it," Foote states (Wood, SBTS). Wood, who agrees that many of Foote's characters are seeking familial acceptance on both earthly and spiritual levels, sums up Foote's understated approach: "redemption is a matter of connection . . . not transcendence" (SBTS).

Along with the Southern protestant religion to which Foote refers here and in his work, notice must be given to the Southern culture in which Foote was brought up and those Southern writers who influenced his approach to writing, both thematically and stylistically. Foote acknowledges the "strong oral tradition" of the South, the appreciation for old family legends passed from one generation to another; "I just took it all in" (Edgerton 4), he laughs. His themes of homecoming and family reconciliations align him with many other Southern writers, especially Katherine Anne Porter, whom Foote respects for her "enormous influence" on his work; Porter and Foote share an appreciation for all the old family stories and utilize them in their writing. Eudora Welty he admires "extravagantly" (Wood, *LFQ* 226), and both Flannery O'Connor and William Faulkner, as well, of whose short stories he has written adaptations. Indeed, Foote's creation of Harrison, the thinly disguised Wharton, is not unlike Faulkner's more famous Jefferson and Yoknapatawpha County.

Further connections could be cited between Foote's work and that of other Southern writers, but one especially should be noted: James Agee, whose own search for reconciliation with a father in his *Death in the Family* Foote both understands and admires (Personal communication 7/28/89). Not only does Agee highlight, as Foote does, the "chain of flesh" that connects the present generation with the past, both writers have dedicated much of their work to honoring their fathers and illustrate in their writing the vital impact a father has on his son and the void that is created when the father is taken away. Although Foote has widened his net of appreciation to include writers of all regions of the world, including poetry along with drama and fiction, his roots in the Southern soil of influence have not withered.

This study has been divided into chapters categorized by dramatic forms, each concentrating on the various stages in Foote's career: early plays, adaptations, original screenplays, the nine-play cycle, and the final one-acts. Further details concerning their composition have been outlined as the works themselves are discussed. In all these, the theme of fathers and their families and the need for reconciliation and homecoming on the human and often spiritual levels will be emphasized, as it is the brightest thread that runs through the tapestry of Foote's canon, lending insight into the man and his vision.[4]

Notes

1 Dr. Gerald Wood is chairman of the English Department at Carson-Newman College in Tennessee.

2 Dr. Terry Barr, a former student of Wood, completed his dissertation at the University of Tennessee.

3 Edgerton is on staff at Goucher College.

4 Although this study follows a general chronological organization, occasionally it is necessary to discuss works out of time-order to maintain continuity in the examination of genres. This slight detouring from Foote's time-line is insignificant as the purpose of this study is not to focus on the development of the playwright or his growth as a writer; rather, the point is to highlight a single theme prevalent in all of Foote's work, from the first available for study to the last.

Chapter Two

"Always Doing Texas": The Early Plays

A brief outlining of Foote's first plays illustrates Foote's early interest in his personal family background and the theme of fathers and their families, though many of the initial works are unavailable for study at this time and Foote's recollections of the pieces will have to suffice here. The early plays, most of which are one-acts, written through the 1950's exhibit an optimistic, even simplistic at times, perspective on life, a view that many of Foote's contemporaries seemed to share at that time. This chapter will examine chronologically as many of the early works as are available.

The shock treatment that society suffered in the 1960's as a result of such traumas as the Viet Nam War, the race riots of the Civil Rights Movement, or, later, the Watergate scandal led Foote, along with many other writers, to reject an innocent or naive life-view for a more sophisticated perspective. Although Foote's understanding of society may have darkened, however, his compassionate concern for his characters did not diminish, nor did his belief in the basic verities of life waver. One sees this most clearly in the later works of his career, to be examined in the final chapter of this study.

Foote recalls coming to the one-act form early in his career as an actor and remembers being impressed by the way in which the playwrights he was reading "strictly observed the unities of time, place, and action. I know now," he relates, "that part of the impact of the play came from the author's skillful use of these unities" (Wood ix); most of Foote's early plays observe these unities, and his utilization of the well-made play form, with its classically developed action from beginning to end, mirrors his perception of a "well-made" world.

Foote began his professional career when he joined the American Actors Theatre (AAT) as an actor. He was initiated into play writing under the encouragement of director Mary Hunter, who was impressed by Foote's skill at dialogue improvisation. Twenty-five years old, he relied on memories of his hometown to create his initial one-act, *Gulf Storm*. The play was produced in the 1939-40 season, under the new title of *Wharton Dance*, and starred Foote himself (Barr 27). Today, Foote half-jokingly admits he became a playwright for the sole purpose of making "sure there was a leading part for myself!" (Calio 76) *Texas Town*, the next play Foote wrote for the company, was a full-length play also derived from his personal hometown history and also starred the playwright. Neither of these two early plays was published or is available for current study. Produced in 1940-41, *Texas Town* did receive good reviews from New York *Times* theatre critic Brooks Atkinson for honestly presenting the "truths of small-town life." At least according to this leading theatre critic, Foote's view of the world as he knew it and as exhibited in his plays was clear-eyed and widely accepted. Foote claims that Atkinson's review did much to establish him as a playwright, as well as influence him to give up acting, as the critic did not laud the lead performer! (Barr 28)

Foote returned to the one-act form in a series of four related one-acts under the blanket title of *Out of My House*, produced by the AAT during the 1941-42 season. Although this work is also unavailable for study, Foote writes that "all of these plays were an exploration of a town and its people that I was to continue over the years. I began by using the name of the Texas town I was born in [Wharton]," he admits, "but the literalness of it was too confining to me, so I renamed it Harrison, and much of my writing life . . . has been spent in this mythical town" (Wood x). Later, Foote was to collect several of these early one-acts in an anthology he called *Harrison, Texas*.

Only the Heart, Foote's first published work, enjoyed both an off-Broadway run in 1943 and a Broadway production in 1944. A full-length play, it immediately demonstrates Foote's concern for the family and examines specifically the difficulties a child experiences when either neglected by its father or manipulated by its mother. This particular concentration recurs in many of the later plays and suggests what Foote sees as the root of many family problems. When love between a parent and child is stifled, authority figures are confused, or when materialism replaces well-developed relationships between family members as family priorities, the entire family suffers. When fathers are absent or too passive to carry their share of the responsibility, forcing mothers to take on the roles of both mother and father, the child especially is the victim.

Mamie Borden is the domineering mother in *Only the Heart*, who has worked hard, sacrificing quality time with her daughter Julia to give her the material things she never had herself. Now that Julia is on the threshold of adulthood, Mamie longs to recapture the lost time, becoming an intruding stranger in her daughter's life. Julia eventually marries the man her mother chooses, but when it becomes clear that Mrs. Borden's manipulation of her daughter and son-in-law's lives has only just begun, the newlyweds escape the Borden household to initiate their own life together.

Only the Heart takes its title from a line of Heinrich Heine's poetry: "They flourish and flourish from year to year/And only the heart is left withered and sere." At the end of the play, Mamie is left alone; as the call comes that her oil wells have come in, she announces emptily to no one, "We're rich" (72). Though Mamie's material well-being flourishes, her heart could not be more withered; and though she has manipulated to gain more than she could ever need, she lacks the only thing she really wanted, a family. Foote's commentary on family relationships comes through unmistakably clear and well-defined, even in this early play.

Foote's insight into the motivation behind such parents as Mamie Borden and his compassion for their situation, however, is equally suggested in *Only the Heart*, a testament to this budding element unique in Foote's work. To explain Mrs. Borden's actions, the play recalls her own neglected childhood in which she had to fend for herself without parental love, thus developing a manipulative spirit. Needing to be resourceful to survive, Mamie has ignored her own need for a family and allowed work to replace any affection in her life. In the end, Mamie Borden is to be pitied, rather than despised, as she is left abandoned without even her husband's company.

Mamie's ambitious lifestyle and her inability to demonstrate affection have driven her husband to another woman for solace. Though Mrs. Borden tries to keep her husband's affair secret from their daughter, she worries that their failed marriage will have a negative effect on Julia and restricts any form of intimacy between the father and child. The parents' problems do have disturbing effects on the daughter. Julia muses: "My mama. My papa. I don't understand them" (67). Having never been allowed to love her father, she has missed out on any love and guidance he could have given her to temper the twisted affection and teaching of her mother. It is only when her father explains their family mistakes that Julia is able to break free of her mother's misguided and suffocating embrace. Though Foote understands and explains Mamie's position, the play makes it clear that Julia's well-being is of the greater importance. This stand in favor of the child is illustrated and championed over and over in most of Foote's following plays.

Only the Heart, the first of Foote's plays available for examination, demonstrates Foote's early roots in the development and maintenance of realism in American theatre. A foreword by Mary Hunter, who served on the executive committee of the AAT of which Foote was Executive Director, was printed with the script in which the purpose of the AAT was defined. Recalling the "primary intention" of the AAT was to uncover "our own cultural roots" (5), Hunter announced that "one of the most gratifying achievements of the American Actors Theatre has been the development of Horton Foote as a playwright." Citing her own program note for one of Foote's plays, Hunter explained: "It does not seem that our kind of theatre should serve as the medium for intellectual analysis or strive to present economic schemes; but rather that it should fuse elements of flesh and blood experience and try through emotional transfer to open the audience's own understanding" (6).

This awareness of purpose allows the modern reader or audience a deeper insight into the style of play writing which has become Foote's home: truly realistic drama that reproduces as faithfully as possible real life situations, settings, and language, in the tradition of such theatre greats as Ibsen and Chekhov; it is a theatre of "flesh and blood" in the "real language of men," to borrow Wordsworth's phrase.

The one-act play was seeming to "lose favor" in New York, and as "no one wanted to produce one-acts," Foote reasoned, "it seemed futile to write them" (Barr x). He attempted a three-month bout in 1944 with screen writing for Universal Studios in Hollywood, but the commercially profitable but intellectually suffocating "formula writing" was not his forte. He returned to New York in 1944 to write the one-act dance plays *Daisy Lee* and *The Lonely*, as well as *Miss Lou* and *Good-bye to Richmond*.[1]

Before the year was out, Foote and his wife Lillian Vallish moved to Washington, D. C., where he was to teach acting and writing, while founding a theatre workshop at the King-Smith School of the Creative Arts. Here, he continued to write and produce his own work, including *Homecoming*, *People in the Show*, and *Themes and Variations*. None of these plays was published or is available for current study, but Foote recalls abandoning in many of these one-acts "the unities of time and place that I had imposed upon my earlier one-acts." Older and wiser in his experience with the world, Foote reveals his maturity in these plays by adding "many scenes and a much more complicated time scheme." He claims he "continued this approach in the plays I did for television in the 1950's" (Wood x).

Foote's initiation into writing for television stems from his relationship with a fellow actor, Vincent Donehue, with whom he had co-founded the King-Smith School in Washington. Although by 1948 Foote had returned to New York to teach at the American Theatre School, this friendship with Donehue led Foote to work at NBC where Fred Coe, Donehue's college roommate, was executive producer of Television Playhouse. According to Terry Barr's discussion of the "Golden Age" of television of the 1940's and 1950's, Coe "was in many ways the inspiration and driving force behind television's live drama period" (52). In the preface to his 1955 collected teleplays, *Harrison, Texas*, Foote praises Coe's attitude toward writers:

> Coe believes deeply in writers, and his belief, in turn, gives the writer a feeling of confidence . . . A play was cast, not for the commercial value of some Broadway or Hollywood name, but with the actors who could best serve the play. . . . If changes in the plays were asked for, one knew that they were not to please some sponsor or advertising agency but rather for the good of the production. . . . In nearly all instances . . . the writer . . . was left free to do his job as best he could (viii).

Unlike the television programming of today, which is geared to entertain the masses, during its infant days of the 1940's and early 1950's television was aimed at producing a higher quality of material for the better-educated audience who could afford television sets. Half-hour and full-hour short story anthology shows dominated the airwaves in those early days, relying on original, thought-provoking scripts from some of America's most talented writers.[2]

The first play Foote was to offer Coe, a short one-act entitled *The Rocking Chair*, continues Foote's focus on family, but expands the definition of family to include one's community and illustrates the view of the father-figure fulfilling his responsibility to his community-family even at the risk of personal sacrifice. The play portrays the small-town doctor White Ewing, whose position as pillar of his community impedes his plans of retirement. A strong sense of commitment, laced with compassion, will not allow the doctor to abandon these "country people who need me and trust me" (21), and he gives in their demands to remain useful to his "family."

As *Only the Heart* provides insight into its character's motivations, this play explains why Dr. Ewing's fatherly role is not restricted to his personal family alone but expanded to cover the large community-family he has given his lifetime to protect. Although unable to save the life of his own daughter, Dr. Ewing has counter-balanced his personal failure with his ability to save the lives of others' children. By losing himself in his care for his other patients, he has been able to survive his personal loss, thus exchanging sorrow with hope and affirming Foote's suggestion that only through loving one's neighbor does one find full satisfaction in life. This point illustrates Foote's definition of several words key to his theme: family, father, and love; it also suggests a connection between earthly and spiritual implications in Foote's works as it echoes the well-known Biblical command: "Love thy neighbor."

The play ends, highlighting both father-related roles the doctor has played, as he promises to drive his wife out to the cemetery where their daughter is buried. This physical act of remembering loved ones with carved tombstones and graveyard visits is one that is repeated over and over in Foote's work, as well as in his own life. Throughout Foote's canon, it is a concrete illustration of the sometimes wordless emotion that exists between parents and their children.

Although *The Rocking Chair* did not meet Coe's needs, Donehue furthered Foote's involvement in television through an introduction to Martin Stone, the producer of The Gabby Hayes Show, where Foote was to work for two seasons. Foote was commissioned, also, by the *Lamp Unto My Feet* religious television series to write a play, which aired on February 4, 1951 as *Ludie Brooks*.

Ludie Brooks provides an interesting contrast to *The Rocking Chair*, highlighting the grief a father feels when he has lost a child. In this case, the father is a Methodist preacher, and, like Dr. Ewing, another father-figure in the eyes of the community. Unlike Dr. Ewing, though, who found peace when his daughter died by immersing himself in giving care to his community, Ludie Brooks has collapsed under the weight of his loss. Not only has he failed in his role as minister and neglected the needs of his church, Ludie has also lost his own faith in God.

Feeling betrayed by this Father-figure in his life, he is as grief-stricken by the crisis in his faith as he is over the death of his child. The community is equally stunned by the absence of their minister-father, as news of Ludie's condition reaches the church. It is only when confronted by a church member who counsels her preacher with what she has learned about faith from her own experience that Ludie's faith is renewed and his grief abated. Relinquishing his will to God's will, he finds the strength to shoulder the fatherly responsibilities of both his personal family and his church family, realizing, like Dr. Ewing in *The Rocking Chair*, that a father's duty to his "family" is to continue working in the land of the living, being in proper submission to his heavenly Father.

Ludie Brooks calls attention again to the community and family, affirming the promise of personal fulfillment through one's compassionate role in that unit. The spiritual element that rises to the forefront of this play is an early indication, too, of Foote's connecting human relationships with spiritual ones more prominent in later works. *Ludie Brooks* intimates that unless one's relationship is right with God, his relationship with the family of man will struggle; however, of equal importance, unless one's faith is of practical use, it is of little good in the family unit.

After *Ludie Brooks*, Coe soon approached Foote for original teleplays for his Philco/Goodyear Theatre, and on April 27, 1952, *The Travellers* was produced. A full-length play, *The Travellers* is unique in Foote's canon as it is set in New York City in the 1950's. The action centers around two young women from Richmond, Texas, who have come to the big city to locate eligible men. The play illustrates Foote's philosophy that children with good relationships with their fathers are more likely to mature into successful and happy adults than children with uninterested fathers.

The self-sufficient, sophisticated Sue Stella has had to earn everything she has by years "of poundin' a typewriter"; her trip ends in disaster when she falls in love with a married man. Nadine, the less experienced but more family-nurtured girl, discovers a secure and happy future with a young serviceman as the result of her vacation. Fatherless, Sue Stella points out that Nadine's father has always taken care of his daughter, even paying for her trip to New York. "I don't have any daddy with oil wells," she reminds Nadine. While it is a minor point that one father can supply luxuries for his daughter while another daughter has to fend for herself, the situation is common to many of Foote's plays. As Nadine appears to be better cared for than Sue Stella and her trip proves to be more successful than her less fortunate friend's,

Foote's suggestions of the effect of a father's concern for his child should not be overlooked. Things seem to work out better for the child with the caring parent.

The friction between parents and children, particularly fathers and their sons, concerning the choice of a profession surfaces often in Foote's plays; sometimes the child is forced to make a clean, but painful break with his family in order to mature as an individual and realize his dreams. Julia Borden in *Only the Heart*, exemplifies such a courageous individual. More timid sons and daughters find themselves acquiescing to bullying parents' wishes, giving up any chance of ever achieving a life of their own, as several later plays illustrate. Occasionally, the parents eventually recognize their child is no longer their "baby" and allow the young adult to attain his dream.

Fortunately this final description seems to be the case with John Rogers, the young serviceman Nadine befriends in *The Travellers*. He reveals to her his problems of getting along with his father, a respected lawyer, who was not pleased when John quit law school for the service. On his last night in New York, however, John's father flies in unexpectedly to spend some time with his son, suggesting their reconciliation and ending the play on an optimistic note. Once again, Foote is careful at least to intimate the promise of healed relationships between parents and children, and *The Travellers* is exemplary of Foote's suggestion of the proper bonding between fathers and their sons and daughters.

Gerry Wood has collected many of Foote's one-acts in a volume published in 1989. The first play in Wood's collection, *The Old Beginning*, was the next play Foote created for Coe in 1952.[3] Set in Harrison, Texas, *The Old Beginning* continues this theme of conflict between father and son that was introduced in *The Travellers*. In *The Old Beginning*, Tommy Mavis has lived his twenty-three years under his father's domineering thumb, helping with his father's rental business but never allowed to take any initiative with the father-son enterprise.

The play opens on the eve of Tommy's attempt at a beginning of his own when he contracts to rent the building his father has just given him. That Tommy is starting his new business on left-overs from his father's is noteworthy and foreshadows further conflict in the play, as Tommy has yet to make a clean break with his father. Mr. Mavis demonstrates he has no intention of giving his son free-reign, though, and when approached by a stranger to rent the building, Mavis closes the deal, unaware of his son's action. "I make all the business arrangements for him," Mavis insists. "He's only a youngster." When father and son discover the other's contracts, each insists the other back down. Eventually, unable to convince his father of the necessity of his independence, Tommy strikes out on his own, not unlike Julia in *Only the Heart*.

Not only is this altercation between Mavis and his son repeated similarly in other Foote work, Foote implies that such friction between fathers and children is common, if not inevitable, throughout society. When a shocked Mrs. Mavis cries, "To think a father and son can't get along" (40), her son answers wisely, "It happens all the time." Tommy has awakened to the knowledge that the incident between him and his father is part of the ritual of letting go that must occur between parents and children, age and youth. While this tug-of-war between father and son adds to the comic element of the play, it underscores the dominance of the old man over the child. That the conflict is truly an "old" beginning becomes obvious when Mrs. Mavis reveals that Tommy's father's "father was the same way. So was mine" (14), intimating that this ritual is the cycle all parents and their children are forced to repeat.

Foote leaves his audience with the knowledge that the severing of parental ties is a necessary pain if children are ever going to have lives of their own, but one for which there is almost certainly the hope of reconciliation further down the road. Tommy's fiancee assures him that someday his parents will understand why he "had to win" (46). In these early plays, at least, family intentions are well-meaning, love exists even if it is obscured, and hope for reunions is promised.

Wood writes in his introduction to *A Young Lady of Property*, that "in *The Old Beginning* Tommy Mavis needs to go away from home in order to gain his autonomy and, hopefully, his identity. He is a pilgrim. But Wilma Thompson's desire to 'get rich and famous' is a flight from failed intimacy" (48). Wilma is the fifteen-year-old protagonist of the Foote's next play, *A Young Lady of Property* (1953), set in Harrison in the year of 1925.[4]

The "failed intimacy" Wood suggests is the disconnected bond between Wilma and her widowed father. Foote paints a sobering portrait of a father-child relationship that suffers from misunderstanding and lack of love. Ever since her mother died, Wilma's father has ignored his daughter, requiring his sister Gert to care for the abandoned child. Wilma reciprocates her father's neglect with negative feelings, even blaming him for the death of her mother whom she adored. As her father prepares to remarry, Wilma plans to go to Hollywood to become a movie star, rather than watch another woman usurp her mother's position.

Foote does not make clear whether Mr. Thompson's neglect of his daughter stems from grief over his wife's death, but the probability of such motivation is implied. Again, Foote provides an insight into the possibility, softening the harsh portrait painted of an uncaring father. Mr. Thompson's need for love and acceptance is exhibited in his desire to marry Mrs. Leighton. It is unnatural to hate one's father, even in spite of the substantial cause Wilma may have, Foote implies, too. He uses Wilma's best friend, Arabella Cookenboo, a child who is cared for by both parents, to demonstrate the ideal family situation and to serve as a foil to Wilma's bitterness against her father. The play goes on to reveal Wilma's hatred is actually a defense mechanism against Mr. Thompson's indifference. Later she admits to loving her father instead and claims, "Maybe I was going to Hollywood out of pure lonesomeness. I felt so alone with Mrs. Leighton getting my daddy and my mama having left the world." Unable to confide in her father who is preoccupied by his new romance, Wilma tells Arabella, "Daddy could have taken away my lonesomeness, but he didn't want to" (70).

The contrast between a house, an empty structure, and a home, a loving family unit, is one that Foote's plays often illustrate. Wilma, who lacks a family, tries to comfort herself with the knowledge that she owns her own house, the one her mother left her when she died. She masks her hurt and fear through a feigned disinterest and dislike for both her father and his fiancee, pathetically trying to lose herself in dreams of Hollywood and pride in the ownership of this house. Attempting to replace her desire for a real family "home" with an attachment to a "house," she brags to Arabella about being a "young lady of property" at the tender age of fifteen. When Arabella retorts that she has a house, too, Wilma insists that just living in a house is not the same as owning one. That Arabella's house is actually a home peopled with a loving family, while Wilma's house is empty of all but wistful memories, accentuates Foote's championing a "home" over a "house," the recurring symbol in many of his plays.

It is only when Wilma's father attempts to sell the house that Wilma's true desires for a family are exposed: "What kind of luck is it takes your mama away, and then your daddy, and then tries to take your house?" (79), she mourns. In desperation, she confronts her father and his fiancee. Naturally, Mrs. Leighton is not the monster Wilma's injured feelings have created her to be; she promises to become a caring step-mother to Wilma, convincing Mr. Thompson to see Wilma's position. The play describes their emotional reconciliation; Wilma's father even invites his daughter to his wedding and to visit him and his bride in Houston. Her family somewhat restored, Wilma claims, "I don't feel nearly so lonely, now I've got my house. . . . And my daddy and I are going to see each other, and I think Mrs. Leighton is going to make a nice friend" (86).

As in most of the early plays, Foote creates a positive ending for his characters, healing whatever wounds have been inflicted between family members. He even suggests that "most people are nice once you get to know them" and deals compassionately with even his hardest characters. It would be negligent, however, to overlook the pathos in Wilma's situation. Her father has agreed to include her in his life, only at the request of his new bride, and then only at a distance. And although Wilma's house has been returned to her, even she realizes that a house is not a home. Sitting on the porch of her

"Always Doing Texas": The Early Plays

house with Arabella, she has not been able to exorcise all the ghosts of her past, lonely life:

> I felt funny there for a minute. A cloud passed over the moon and I felt lonely . . . I remember one night Aunt Gert woke me up. . . . she was crying. "I'm taking you home to live with me . . . Because your mama's gone to heaven," she said. (A pause.) I can't remember my mama's face anymore. I can hear her voice sometimes calling me far off: "Wilma, Wilma, come home." Far off. But can't remember her face. . . . Oh, Arabella. It isn't only the house I wanted. It's the life in the house. My mama and me and even my daddy coming in at four in the morning . . . (87).

Foote would be remiss, however, in this early play if he allowed the scene to end on such an uncertain and poignant note. Wilma and her father are reconciled, and Foote suggests the possibility for growth between the two in the future. Arabella reminds Wilma that "there'll be life again in the house [because] you'll fill it with life again" (87), and we hear Aunt Gert, Wilma's substitute mother, calling for her to come home, just as her mother used to do. And lest we doubt that Foote intended the security these words imply, his final stage directions make the suggestion definitive: "Wilma looks happy and is happy as the lights fade" (87). Whatever personal cynicism the audience may bring to the production is reduced by the evidence of a happy ending in this early Foote piece.

Wilma has had to grow up and accept the reality of her "half-orphaned" situation, even as she realizes the budding of many of her dreams. In the Preface to his *Harrison* collection, Foote wrote that his plays share "an acceptance of life or a preparation for death" (viii). This theme of coming to terms with what one already has in the fellowship of the community or the richness of the land continues in several of these works. *The Oil Well* (1953) is exemplary of Foote's explanation of what many of his plays have in common.[5] It also continues the portrayal of fathers who have failed to provide for their children as they had hoped. In *The Oil Well*, Foote implies that this failure has been brought on by a misplacement of a father's faith from his religion and land to seductive but disappointing "get rich quick" schemes: Will attempts to give up his farm land for the possibility of discovering oil on his property.

Wood writes in his preface to the play, "'the substance of [Will's] faith' has become oil, the new religion, and the only justification of his new values will be his acquisition of wealth" (90). He further intimates that as Will substitutes his old faith with a new "worship of money," he neglects the best interests of his family, erroneously believing that more money is a greater inheritance for his children than love and his attempts to provide for them through hard work.

Foote leads the audience to equate this love of money with a new god that people like Will are foolishly worshipping by creating several comparisons between Will's activities and traditional religious symbols or phrases: he has Will dressed in his "Sunday suit" to close the deal and has him call the discovery of oil on his land a "prophecy [that] has come true." Will also refers to his good fortune as the revelation of a "sign and a plan," and several references are made to Will's new "faith." Will even questions his wife and daughter's hesitancy to believe in the oil scheme with "Where's your faith? I swear. What kind of a family do I have? My wife has no faith and my daughter . . ." (100). His daughter replies that she does have faith, but her faith is no longer in her father since he has replaced his more fundamental beliefs with the new oil god.

The play suggests that a family is required to support a father's outlook only when it is well-grounded in old and proven mores; when a father loses his grip on fundamental values, the family can either follow to its own ruin or break its faith with the father. In *Oil Well*, both the children and the mother listen to reason to provide for themselves, abandoning Will to his own misguidedness. While Foote's sympathies are undoubtedly with the mother and children, ever understanding and compassionate with his characters, however, Foote clearly presents Will's intentions as pure: he wants the fortune his oil will bring in order to better his family's standard of living. He enumerates the material conveniences he plans to purchase for his wife and children.

Through Will, Foote calls attention to society's blind preference of material gain over simple love and concern for one's family. He also demonstrates how the responsibility of a father to provide for his family can be overwhelming, as Will remembers the drudgery of their own past life and longs to break the cycle of having to work hard to eke out a mere passable living. "How many times have I stood this way," he cries, "watched my papa before me, his papa" (115). Confusing his ability to love and provide the necessities for his family with the desire to lavish extravagances on them that society has instilled in him, Will is a "double-minded man, unstable in all his ways," as the book of *James* describes.

The adage that "the love of money is the root of all evil" comes to mind as the relationship between following the false god of money to one's perdition is further delineated in the play when Cousin Mamie hurries in from out of town to celebrate the possibility of her family's good fortune. When the taxi driver questions her rush with "Is there a death in the family?" she aptly replies, "No, there's no death. There's an oil well" (121). It is as though Foote is implying that they lead to the same result.

Indeed Will's inability to discern the valuable leads to the death of his dreams, at least, as his belief in this new faith is drowned in the salt water which is all his "oil wells" seem capable of producing. A defeated man, Will finally relinquishes his misplaced faith and pitifully crawls back to accept the old Truth. "We've got lots to be grateful for," he reminds himself and his wife. "We certainly have fine children" (127). As the children were the focus of his dreams from the very start, Will is able to pick up where he left off. Like Coleridge's wedding guest, he is a "sadder but wiser man," as he returns to the cotton fields with his wife to resume the old ways, the children's true interests and his responsibility to them in clearer focus than before.

While *The Oil Well* may not appear to be as optimistic as most of the earlier plays discussed, the reconciliation of family and the restoration of fundamental values depicted in the end clearly illuminate Foote's view of what is truly important. He has an uncompromised understanding of the ideal family relationship which he holds up in comparison with the reality of relationships he has discovered in his life's experience and which he portrays in his work.

The Death of the Old Man (1953) continues Foote's criticism of misplaced priorities, only this time it is not the father who has failed in grasping what Foote sees as really valuable in life but his sons.[6] This teleplay is unique in Foote's work in that the protagonist, the old man Will Mayfield, is actually the "eye of the camera"; while his face is never seen, everything is viewed from his perspective and his thoughts are revealed through a voice-over.

The old man, on his deathbed, is unafraid to die, but he worries about his daughter Rosa. As Will always believed "in investin' my money in livin' things . . . helpin' the poor . . . . Not in storin' money up in banks'" (135), he has nothing to leave her for her provision. Now, he realizes this lack of material investment may result in Rosa's destitution, as she has dedicated her life to taking care of her father and has been trained for no other work. His well-established sons refuse to provide for their sister. Though they claim they "meant to do our best" (139) and "be like Papa," they insist "times have changed. . . . People can't live that way anymore" (141). When Will realizes he has failed to pass his legacy of generosity on to his sons, he mourns, "Then I've lost. My investment's wasted . . . Kindness has gone from the world" (139, 141), and bitterly wants to die.

In the style of some of the earlier plays, Cousin Lyd, an older woman who runs a country store, arrives like a *deus ex machina* to offer Rosa a home with her. The old man is content to die now, because he is assured his gentle daughter will have security and love, and his faith in the old commitment to family has been restored, even in the face of its demise in the current society his sons now represent. Again, in this early play, Foote reaffirms old values of compassion and restores the likelihood of the triumph of good.

Tears of My Sister (1953) is an interesting companion piece for *The Death of the Old Man* in that it utilizes the "camera's eye" and voice-over mechanisms of the former play.[7] In *Tears of My Sister* the relationship of a father and his family is not so overtly displayed as in the earlier plays, but the emphasis is just as important as it is subtle. The action of the play focuses on the eldest daughter of the Monroe family, Bessie, as she unhappily prepares to wed a wealthy man she does not love so that her mother and younger sister Cecilia can have a secure future. Her actions are the direct result of her father's death two years before; since then, the family has had to fend for itself.

When the father died, Cecilia informs us, her sister "cried then like her heart would break and would never mend in this world.... She still cries when you mention Papa's name" (153-154). Whether Bessie simply enjoyed a loving relationship with her father or whether she realized even then that she would be called upon to make sacrifices for the sake of the family is not spelled out. This situation surfaces again and again in Foote's work, indicating the sacrifices young girls are required to make for their families, either at their fathers' requests or because they need to take on the responsibilities of their absent fathers.

Obviously, the role of a father is a difficult one, as *Oil Well* has suggested, but when a mother or child has to add the paternal burden to her own demanding family role, the result can be overwhelming. Bessie's mother claims that "havin' to be father and mother to us has broken her" (157). When the father is no longer there to provide for his family, even at no fault of his own, the family members themselves are the victims, the play illustrates. The predicament here has caused the mother to turn their home into a boarding house, because "we have to be practical in this world," echoing the difference between houses and homes introduced in *A Young Lady of Property*. With the family unit itself fragmented, the home, broken into rental rooms, serves as a symbol for that destruction.

The plight of the orphan, like that of the abandoned women in *Tears of My Sister* and *A Young Lady of Property*, is another theme dear to Horton Foote's heart. In fact, he dedicates an entire cycle of nine plays, *The Orphans' Home*, to that topic. Wood intimates that in a sense, all of Foote's protagonists are symbolic orphans as they are "haunted by a sense of rootlessness and disconnection that, the playwright feels, is part of the modern sensibility." These characters "crave ties to others, a place to make their own, a sense of identity that brings the peace and contentment we all long for" (168-169). His comments introduce the next play, *John Turner Davis* (1953), and indicate its connection to most of Foote's other works.[8] In this play Foote acknowledges the reality of the absence of his "ideal family" and presents two parts of a puzzle pregnant with positive possibilities for reunion: a loving husband and wife longing for a child to care for and an abandoned child with no one to love.

John Turner Davis, set in Harrison in 1933, fleshes out the portrait of the orphan named in the play's title. Abandoned by his parents at an early age, John Turner has developed a self-discovered wisdom concerning family that exceeds his age: "I've seen the poorest kind of people, with enough kids to make you dizzy thinkin' about it, but try to take one of them kids an' they'd fight you until they killed you or you killed them" (179). He has come to the conclusion that his own parents "must have [not] cared much about me" (179), explaining that they gave him away to be reared by an aunt and uncle.

Often Foote expands his definition of "relative" or "family" to include the extended family who may demonstrate a deeper love than those of the immediate family. This is illustrated by the relationship John Turner claims to have enjoyed with his aunt and uncle. Not only has he observed how most normal parents love their children, as stated above, he feels he has experienced that love through his "foster" parents, his aunt and uncle. Once, when his uncle had to leave them to go find work, "a sheriff come along [he remembers] and says they couldn't raise me right an' he was gonna take me and put me in a home," and his aunt had to fight the authorities off with a gun. Abandoned again, this time by his aunt and uncle, at the beginning of the play John Turner admits that his aunt and uncle have left him to find work; he is confident that they will return to claim him, even though the community believes his "people has just run off and left him."

Thurman and Hazel Whyte, a barren couple in the community who have longed for a child of their own, eagerly offer the orphaned boy a home. Reluctant to replace his aunt and uncle with new "parents," John Turner accepts their offer only temporarily at first. When it becomes clear, however, that he has been abandoned a second time, he swallows his pride and former feelings for his original family to accept the Whytes' invitation. "Now I've got no mama an' papa an' no aunt or uncle," he concludes. "I got 'em, I guess, but I don' know where they are. So might as well not have 'em for all the good they doin' me" (196). The boy matures in his understanding of what makes a family: blood ties have little to do with commitment; parental love for children, even orphans, can come from the larger family, the community, when compassion is present.

Compassion is available even for John Turner's relatives, as Foote provides insight into their situation. Just how much his aunt and uncle really care for John Turner is debatable. While it may be easy to criticize their actions, their motives, as described by John Turner, are surely commendable. For even though they are not the blood parents of the boy, they appear to have a loving commitment to the child which is restricted only by their poverty. John Turner explains their having left him on previous occasions only so that he could be better provided for by some sympathetic but more financially secure couple like the Whytes; their love for the boy always made them return, though. It takes a lot of love on the part of blood relatives to relinquish that relationship for the more stable environment for the child they love; this sacrifice illuminates a deeper meaning of family in Foote's work, perhaps more than in any other discussed thus far.

John Turner also comes to realize the difference between a house and a home, just as Wilma does in *A Young Lady of Property*, only Foote reverses the terms in this play. The boy mentions that the sheriff thinks he would "be better off" in a "home that boys can go to, where they can give you an education and teach you a trade" (196), but he is old enough to understand that this kind of "home" is really just a shelter. What he really wants is to live in the house where foster parents like the Whytes are eager to accept him as their own. When Thurman insists they have longed for a boy of their own and offers John Turner their home, the boy replies, "All my life I wanted to live in a house" (196). In this case, the house is the actual home because love resides there. The lights fade on the new family sitting on the porch, listening to the rain that has come to their parched land ever since John Turner's arrival, a symbol of the love that has grown into a family where there was none. The family bond has been restrengthened and the probability for positive endings is reinforced again.

Wood writes that the next play, *The Midnight Caller* (1953), "if for no other reason, . . . would be important because it was the first play by Horton Foote in which Robert Duvall acted" (199).[9] While this relationship has proved to be vital through the years for both Foote and Duvall, the play itself is interesting to our discussion as it illustrates from a different angle the problems domineering mothers can create for their children, especially when fathers are absent from the home. Set in Harrison in 1952, *The Midnight Caller* offers, as in *Tears of My Sister*, a home that has had to be turned into a boardinghouse where other "homeless" people can find shelter. Here, Helen Crews has retreated to escape the interference of her mother and the drunken affections of Harvey Weems, a boy she once loved but whose weakness for alcohol and his own mother's apron strings has numbed her feelings.

This clinging together of mother and child is a prominent cause of failure in the lives of Foote's characters. Here, unlike Tommy who manages to break the cycle in *The Old Beginning*, several characters have succumbed to this weakness. Miss Rowena, one of many spinster boarders at the house where Helen resides, speaks for many of the unmarried women when she reveals that her own fate was sealed by an over-protective mother who "insisted I stay in my room" while she ran off any would-be suitors. This subconscious reason for the lack of marriage in Harrison is an underlying theme in many of Foote's plays, surfacing again and again to reveal parents who maintain an obsessive hold on their children for one reason or another, keeping them from creating lives of their own. "Too much of a good thing" seems to be Foote's point in regard to mothers who suffocate their children with a selfish love.

Helen, however, suggests this mistake on the part of their mothers has its own deep roots: "And I don't know who to blame. My mother? For wantin' to keep me and my sister locked up with her forever? How can I blame her? We're all she had. My father died when we were just babies. . . . My father lost everything speculating on the cotton market. Maybe my father's to blame" (219). Again, Foote's plays provide understanding insight into characters' personalities, and, as in *Tears of My Sister*, the ultimate responsibility seems to lie with the father, whose role in the family's life is vital to its survival. The absent fathers in *The Midnight Caller* are very present in the sense that their failure to provide a stable relationship with their families has led to the near demise of the family in Harrison.

Proving that she has learned from her experience with her parents and former lover, Helen relinquishes the suicidal Harvey to accept the advances of Ralph Johnston, a new boarder who has proposed to her. Divorced and lonely, he has realized how much he values a family and offers this second chance at happiness to Helen, leading her away from the failure of her former life to a new and hopefully more satisfying one in Houston.

The play itself, however, does not end on such a hopeful note with the drunken Harvey still calling for Helen, as he has done throughout the play, and Miss Rowena answering his plea with whispers he cannot possibly hear, "She's gone, Harvey. Gone to Houston. Gone . . ." (231). For those who do not have the strength or desire to break free of crippling relationships to establish healthier, independent, and more responsible ones, their hope can only be gone. While Foote provides a forgiving look into the backgrounds of such failed characters, his charity toward them cannot overcome the resulting reality of their situations. *The Midnight Caller* joins *Tears of My Sister* in ushering in a less pleasant outlook in future plays depicting the world of Harrison, Texas.

The Dancers (1954), set in Harrison in 1952, further demonstrates the necessity of breaking away from manipulative adults, though this play diverts from the pattern begun with *Tears of My Sister* and *The Midnight Caller* in the sense that the teenagers here are able to achieve their own success.[10] Here, Mrs. Crews, in an attempt to divert her daughter Emily from dating boys she "doesn't approve of" (240), tries to force Emily into a date with young Horace, who has come to Harrison to visit his sister Inez and her husband Herman Stanley. Inez eagerly accepts the role of substitute mother in her attempt to push the shy Horace into a social whirl, as she shares Mrs. Crews' belief that the young people will "thank me someday" (238).

Emily, however, as headstrong as her mother, sidesteps her mother's plans by feigning illness, and Horace, determined not to be manipulated by his sister, befriends another girl, Mary Catherine, whom he takes to the dance, in spite of all the grownups' maneuverings. Like Tommy in *The Old Beginning*, the teenagers realize if they are ever to enjoy lives of their own, they have to walk away from well-meaning but conniving adults.

Foote's illustration of proper father figures is obvious in *The Dancers*. While the mothers exhaust themselves with their unsuccessful schemes, the fathers seem to have leveler heads on their shoulders when it comes to dealing with their children. One example is depicted as Herman, Horace's brother-in-law, finds it necessary to step into the father-role when Inez insists on playing mother to her brother. When Horace makes his own plans, foiling his sister's, Herman chides, "Leave the boy alone. He'll be all right. Only don't push him. You and your mother have pushed the boy and pushed him" (249). Here, Herman suggests the problem behind the problem: as Horace's father, the judge, seems to have little time to devote to his son's upbringing, his mother has made rather unsuccessful attempts at filling the roles of both parents.

Mary Catherine Davis's father best exemplifies a father who knows how to execute his job as a loving, but nonconniving parent. Tom Davis, a mechanic who cannot afford nice clothes or an expensive home, worries that "he can't afford to send [his daughter] to college" (256). Showing how deeply she cares for this man who truly cares for her, Mary Catherine confides in Horace her reason for choosing to attend a local business school instead:

> When I was in seventh grade I thought I would die if I couldn't get there [college], but then when I was in the ninth, Mother talked to me one day and told me Daddy wasn't sleeping at nights for fear I'd be dis-

appointed if he couldn't send me, so I told him the next night I decided I'd rather go to business school. He seemed relieved (256).

While another sacrifice by a child for the sake of a parent is being made in this scene, the emphasis in this play is instead on the concern the father and daughter have for one another. The Davis family illustrates the meaning of true love among its members, not the misplaced manipulative concern found in the Crews or Stanley families. In other scenes, Mr. Davis demonstrates his respect for both Mary Catherine and her mother's feelings, and they respond in like manner. Foote implies that even though the Davis family is not as materially blessed as the other characters, because of their love for each other, they are the wealthiest family in the play. In the end, because of their sensible and compassionate approach to child-rearing, they are the only parents given the privilege of witnessing their children's happiness, as they send the children off to enjoy their evening.

Blind Date, a play written nearly thirty years later and included in Wood's collection, immediately reminds one of *The Dancers*. It, too, concerns young people being forced into social situations by their parents. The point of this play, however, is less that of the old versus the young or manipulative parents being outdone by strong-willed teenagers; instead, it depicts the young Sarah Nancy balking at accepting what is expected of young women of her society. As Wood puts it in his introduction, "the problems in *Blind Date* grow from Sarah Nancy's refusal to accept the traditional role of a woman" (363-364). She is stronger and more self-willed, though, than her predecessor Bessie in *Tears of My Sister* who acquiesced to the requirements of her day, and wins her own way in the end.

The focus in this play is on the role that women were required to play in order to be acceptable in a man's world. While this is not unlike the earlier *Tears of My Sister*, the end result is not nearly so tragic; *Blind Date* is presented as a comedy. Perhaps the difference between the two plays is that Sarah Nancy refuses to give in to such unreasonable requirements for her sex, while Bessie can see no way out of her unpleasant circumstances. Either way, once again the situation is of mothers who attempt to arrange their children's lives, while the sensible suggestions offered by the father-figures in the play are chiefly ignored. The children, opting for the male perspective, have a way of working out their problems for themselves. In these plays, Foote paints a portrait of overbearing mothers and well-meaning fathers whose children choose to follow their father's advice, quiet as it may be.

Lest one should arrive at the wrong conclusion from these former plays, Foote illustrates he is not a sexist in regard to his valuing equally the roles of both parents in one of his last teleplays, *Flight*, written in 1956.[11] *Flight* tells the story of Martha Anderson, whose wishes to marry John Dobbs are forbidden by her domineering father. Even her well-meaning mother bows to the father's will, and her younger sister Verna provides a lot of insight into the family situation when she reveals, "I'd die if Papa was mad at me the way he is at Martha" (108).

Foote has maintained in many previous plays that the role of the father is a complex one, and *Flight* supports that point. Mr. Anderson's duty and desire to provide for and protect his daughter must be tempered with reason. Like many fathers, he both wants the best for his daughter and is convinced that he knows what is best. On the one hand he wisely opposes John Dobbs' wild, unstable ways, but on the other hand he illogically refuses to comprehend why his daughter would prefer marriage over the security of her father's home. Mr. Anderson stubbornly repeats the advice his own father gave to his sisters: "I understand a man wanting to get married, but not a girl. You have everything you need. I'll always be able to take care of you" (111).

While fathers may have difficulty performing their duties reasonably when it comes to their beloved daughters, teenage girls can be equally stubborn and illogical. Martha pretends to go along with her father's demands but has no intention of sacrificing her own plans, having, in fact, already married John Dobbs secretly; she is simply waiting for the opportune time to sneak away with her new husband. When her mother discovers Martha's "escape" plans and accuses Martha of loving "that boy so much that you defy your papa," Martha retaliates with exaggerated teenage emotion, "I hate papa and I hate you . . . You don't love me. You just want to see me miserable" (125). Mrs. Anderson tries to pacify both sides: "It's not the kind of marriage [your father] would have chosen for you, but now it's done, I know he'll take it in stride and just make the best of it" (133), she acquiesces in her daughter's defiance. Mr. Anderson has no choice; for once, he is not in control.

One point *Flight* makes is that sometimes fathers really do know what is best. It is discovered that John Dobbs has already left town, abandoning his young wife, demonstrating that Mr. Anderson truly was a good judge of character. Martha must then either admit defeat and face her father's "I told you so," or she can accept this initiation into adulthood and leave town herself to begin life on her own. In the end, she chooses the second option, unwilling to submit to her father's dominance any longer. Her decision elicits a second point affirmed in the play: the necessity of breaking away from one's childhood in order to develop as a mature human being. Although the circumstances are different for Martha, she chooses the same escape route into adulthood taken by Julia in *Only the Heart* and Tommy in *The Old Beginning*. While Mr. Anderson may have been unreasonable in his desire to shield his daughter forever, his role as mature advisor is upheld in the play. Demanding equal admiration, however, is Martha's decision to become responsible for her own actions, foolish or otherwise, particularly for a young woman of her day.

Foote comments in notes printed with the published script that he chose to set his play in 1915 to illustrate the uniqueness of his protagonist's decision. "Hers is an exodus, a flight that was unusual for a girl of her background and environment then," he writes, explaining the way things have changed in our society. "Today, for good or bad, it is constant" (149). Values are no longer as "fixed and settled" are they were at the turn of the century. He goes on to call attention to the continuation of his prominent theme when he concludes, "My characters are often searching for a town or a home to belong to, or a parent, or a child—all parts of the family" (148-149). It is uncertain, however, at the end of *Flight* whether Martha, or even John Dobbs, will ever find reconciliation and acceptance; *Flight*, for that reason alone, serves as a good bridge between the early plays and the later one-acts to be discussed in chapter six.

Each of these early plays has introduced Foote's focus on the family as his predominant theme and illustrated the roles parents play in their children's lives for good or ill. Sometimes the depiction of the ideal family relationship is explicit; at other times, the desired situation is illuminated against a less desirable example. Throughout all the plays, Foote suggests that the impact of a parent's role on a child's life is significant, particularly the position the father chooses to take. The appeal of Foote's philosophy is borne out by the wide acceptance of his stage plays and teleplays on early television. In later plays, while the theme of family relationships will not alter, the probability for happy endings will diminish, as those plays depict a less secure society.

Foote's career in television might have remained secure if Foote could have maintained the pace at which writers were expected to churn out intelligent, interesting, and original scripts. For such programs alone as Philco-Goodyear Playhouse, Studio One, and Playhouse 90, Foote created twenty-six scripts (Edgerton 5). But there was another uncertainty in the situation with which Foote and other successful scriptwriters had to contend. As television proved it was here to stay, television tycoons began to lower their sights to include programming that would attract a broader audience, complete with advertising that was directed at mass America.

This reversal of vision manifested itself in the decline of the more intellectual anthologies in favor of the formulaic episodic weekly programming so familiar to today's audience. No longer was "the play the thing," and, therefore, no longer was the serious playwright appreciated (Barr 49-52). Foote wrote his last teleplay in 1960, though much of his energy during the mid-to-late 1950's when television was undergoing its metamorphosis was spent outside of television, staging and publishing the old teleplays and writing in other media.

Although he was disappointed, Foote's only comment on the demise of television as he knew it is, "You just have to shut it out of your heart somehow" (Barnouw 36).

Notes

1 Foote created *Daisy Lee* for the choreography of Valerie Bettis; *The Lonely* was choreographed by Martha Graham at the Neighborhood Playhouse. Also for the Playhouse, Foote was commissioned to write *Miss Lou* and *Good-bye to Richmond*, the latter of which was performed also at the Baltimore Museum of Art. All these plays, written in 1944, are unavailable for perusal.

2 Barr's dissertation, "The Ordinary World of Horton Foote," provides additional detail concerning these programs and their writers, especially Foote's role in television. See pages 45-63.

3 *The Old Beginning* was produced on Goodyear Theatre November 23, 1952. Foote also changed the setting from Richmond to Harrison, as he would in most subsequent plays to create a sense of community and continuity.

4 *A Young Lady of Property* aired on Fred Coe's Philco Television in April, 1953. Kim Stanley portrayed Wilma Thompson in her first starring role, one of several parts she would accept in Foote's plays.

5 *The Oil Well* was produced on Goodyear Theatre May 17, 1953.

6 *The Death of the Old Man* was produced on the Gulf Playhouse July 17, 1953.

7 Both *The Death of the Old Man* and *Tears of my Sister* were written at the suggestion of producer Fred Coe and directed by Arthur Penn with whom Foote would collaborate later on a less satisfactory project. *Tears of my Sister* appeared on the Gulf Playhouse August 14, 1953, relying on the voice of Kim Stanley in the "camera's eye" role of Cecilia.

8 Directed by Arthur Penn, *John Turner Davis* aired on the Philco Playhouse November 15, 1953.

9 *The Midnight Caller* was produced on Philco Television Playhouse in December, 1953.

10 *The Dancers* aired on Philco Television Playhouse March 7, 1954.

11 *Flight*, which Wood excludes from his collection because it is a full-length play, starred Kim Stanley as Martha Anderson. The play takes on greater significance when compared with the later *Courtship*, the

fourth play in *The Orphans' Home* cycle, as its story is revised and retold in relation to Elizabeth, the character based on Foote's own mother who considered eloping with a man of whom her father did not approve. Mr. Anderson and Mr. Vaughn, Elizabeth's father, reveal great similarities in both their desire to control and to protect their families. *Courtship* is discussed in chapter five of this study.

Chapter Three

Adapting for a Living

Part I
Foote-prints in Faulkner Films: Adaptations of "Old Man," "Tomorrow," and "Barn Burning"

To Foote, writing original material comes spontaneously. "It's part of breathing, part of my identity." In fact, he admits, "I'd even pay you to let me do it." Adapting someone else's work to stage or screen, however, is more difficult. "To adapt," he continues, "you have to pay me a great deal!" Part of Foote's reluctance here comes from his realization that adapting requires "taking on someone else's identity and submerging yourself in it. While you don't have to feel it is great literature, you do have to be sympathetic toward it" (Personal communication 11/14/87).

At first, Foote was not sympathetic to the idea of translating any other writer's work from one medium to another: he had work of his own that needed his time, and when the financial necessity arose for him to adapt "the words and ideas of another author while putting his own ideas on hold indefinitely [it] was a devastating blow" (Barr 127). But neither Hollywood nor Broadway, whose visions were becoming more and more commercialized in the late 1950's and early 1960's, seemed interested in producing the relatively unknown Foote's original material. They were confident, however, in Foote's ability to adapt successfully the works of writers with wider reputations than his own.

Successful is probably not the best adjective to describe Foote's initial attempt at adaptation, in 1955-56: Clinton Seeley's novel, *Storm Fear*. The film received indifferent reviews, confirming Foote's own indifferent attitude to his new role. As

Storm Fear is out of circulation and the screenplay is unavailable, nothing more can be said concerning Foote's "maiden" adaptation experiment.

In a interview with Calvin Skaggs for *The American Short Story*, Foote described film adaptation as the process of "enter[ing] another writer's terrain, and tak[ing] on the beat of another writer's heart" (329). The author next offered to Foote for an adapting assignment, the first in whose "terrain" Foote felt at home, was William Faulkner. Because of his affinity with the Southern writer, whom Foote cites as his greatest literary influence (Personal communication 4/87), Foote swallowed his distaste for adaptation and accepted the assignment.

It is in Foote's adaptations, first of Faulkner's work and then later, Harper Lee's, that Foote's unique contributions to screen writing are especially manifested. Every work's original focus is shifted to concentrate on family, particularly the father-son relationship, and in every work Foote deals compassionately with the characters, putting an emphasis on their development more than on the plot. Finally, Foote's optimistic view of society uplifts even the more jaded pieces, causing the adaptations to exhibit a positive perspective.

Foote's first experience in adapting Faulkner's work came in 1958, when he agreed to rework Faulkner's novella, "Old Man." Three separate adaptations of his short story, "Tomorrow," followed: the first, a teleplay, in 1960; the second, a stageplay, in 1963; and the third, a screenplay, in 1972. "Barn Burning," the last (to date) Faulkner story on which Foote has worked, was not adapted until 1980. Because Foote's translating of Faulkner's work to screen covers three separate works in five projects, they will be discussed together in this section. On each of the pieces Foote left his signature but remained true to the original manuscript; in at least two of the adaptations the emphasis on family and the father-son relationship especially shines through.

In the article, "On First Dramatizing Faulkner," Foote recalls coming to Faulkner's work during the 1940's when it was still relatively unappreciated.[1] Foote became an avid reader of Faulkner material, considering himself "in some measure a student of his then existing work" (50). Fred Coe first offered Foote the opportunity to dramatize Faulkner's *The Sound and the Fury*, but Foote wisely refused on the grounds that "the unique qualities of the work" might not be preservable in a television script. He later agreed to take on Faulkner's "Old Man" for Coe's Playhouse 90, despite misgivings concerning the physical scope of the plot (Foote, "On First Dramatizing Faulkner" 50-51). The novella describes a convict's assignment to rescue a pregnant woman from a flooding Mississippi river (the metaphorical "old man") and to return safely to prison.[2]

As it was his first attempt to dramatize someone else's material, Foote was "very wary of getting involved"; a comparison of both versions of "Old Man" reveals Foote's careful adherence to Faulkner's plot. Foote recalls viewing his task as simply giving dramatic order to the story's chaotic journey, from the convict's orders to take the boat and find the woman, through their encounters with dead animals, snakes, people on other boats, attempts to surrender, the birth of the baby, a sojourn with a Cajun alligator hunter, and to the eventual return to prison.

It was his attraction to the characters, however, that led Foote to immerse himself in Faulkner's world, a world to which he was no stranger, having been reared himself on the Gulf coast of Texas (Foote, "On First Dramatizing Faulkner" 51). Of particular interest to him was the character of the woman: "I never tired thinking of the woman," Foote muses. "She was always (and remains so) a delight to me . . . I wanted as soon as possible to establish a specific character for the woman. I made her a talker and gave her a detailed history" (54-55).

Here Foote's "Old Man" first departs from Faulkner's and takes on characteristics common to Foote's own work. Faulkner's story narrates the psychological and physical journey of the tall convict via monologue, giving little attention to the other characters; on the other hand, Foote's development of the woman creates a growing relationship requiring more vital dialogue between her and the man and shifting the perspective of the story from the one male character to both the convict and the woman. It also allows for Foote's typical focus on "family" that the Faulkner work ignores or even shuns.

Foote's reduction of Faulkner's convict's interior monologue may be explained by the very nature of the necessary reliance on exterior dialogue in a television script. However, monologue (interior or otherwise) is vitally important in most Faulkner works, while dialogue-developed relationships characterize nearly all of Foote's plays.[3] Therefore, the difference in style in the two versions becomes more distinct, indicating Foote's particular, though subtle, mark on Faulkner's "Old Man."

Foote's use of dialogue allows a more caring relationship to develop between the woman and the convict, completely changing the tone of the story. Through his narrative, Faulkner's convict reveals a desperate desire to escape from the real world he has been swept into on the metaphorical "birth canal" of the flooding river to return to the protective "womb" of the penitentiary. From the moment he realizes he is "doomed from the very start never to get rid" of this pregnant woman, whose condition becomes to him a symbol of the nature of all women, "all in the world [he] wants is just to surrender" (Faulkner, "Old Man" 527).

He speaks to her only when necessary and then, irritably. When they are beset by snakes, he longs to shut out her steady shrieking. "Hush!" he demands. "I wish I was a snake so I could get out too!" (536) When finally rid of the woman and back in the cocoon of his cell, he listens to the other convicts' vague sexual fantasies and compares their talk with his actual experience of "woman trouble." Faulkner's comical irony reaches a climax when, once back at the prison farm where he is mistakenly punished for trying to escape, the convict gratefully accepts his "ten more years . . . without no female companionship" (579).

Although Foote's convict experiences the same disappointment when he discovers that the only woman he has had the chance to be alone with since his incarceration is heavily pregnant, unlike Faulkner's convict, he apparently comes to care about her, holding civil and easy conversation with her, calling her "ma'am," and even participating in the naming of her baby. When told he will have to leave the Cajun's cabin where he and the woman have taken refuge before it is dynamited, Foote's convict objects to being deprived of his restored freedom and the "home" he and the woman have created together. "Get away from me," he commands the officers. "You're not taking me any place. . . . I'm not ready to leave here yet. I want to stay here for a while, and work for myself" (Foote, "Old Man" 39).

Later, when the motorboat pilot asks if the woman and convict are related, the woman replies, "Just friends," and they continue to discuss their experience as a trip they have "enjoyed" together. As she contemplates the seven years the convict still has to serve in the penitentiary, the woman muses, "Seven years is not such a long time," implying she considers him worth her wait (42-43).

Still later, back in prison with the ten years added to his sentence for "escaping," Foote's convict admits missing his freedom: "I reckon I'd done forgot how good it was to work for yourself" (47) and ignores the plump convict's suggestive remarks about female companionship as he sits quietly smoking, staring out into the darkness. Though this slight yearning for freedom does not necessarily indicate that Foote's convict desires a relationship with the woman and an eventual family of their own, Foote's "Old Man" does exemplify the gentlemanly nature of Foote's style, an explicit change in tone from Faulkner's piece, and exhibits the charity Foote tends to show his characters, even hardened criminals. The possible promise of an eventual family when the convict is released also lends a hopeful note to Foote's adaptation that Faulkner's work denies.

When "Old Man" aired in September 1958, Foote's adaptation received an Emmy nomination. More important, Foote heard that Faulkner "liked what I did with 'Old Man'" (Personal communication 11/14/87). What Foote did with Faulkner's "Old Man" was to personalize it, civilize it; in so doing, Foote was to remain as true as he felt the other author's work would allow to what was becoming his predominant theme of the importance of the family. Faulkner's "Old Man" may be the more psychologically interesting and is certainly the more comical, but Foote's creates and examines more intimately the relationships between the two characters, offering a more positive portrait for his audience.

Unlike the film version of "Old Man," which has received little critical discussion since its debut, Foote's second Faulkner adaptation, "Tomorrow," has received more acclaim.[4] Both Faulkner's "Tomorrow," one of the stories in the detective collection, *Knight's Gambit*, and Foote's adaptations for television in 1960, the stage in 1963, and film in 1972 reveal cotton-farmer Jackson Fentry's reasons for refusing to acquit the justified killer of ruffian Buck Thorpe. However, while Faulkner focuses on the details of Gavin Stevens' investigation of the mysterious motive behind Fentry's "hanging the jury," Foote concentrates on the relationship between Fentry and the unnamed, "black-complected" woman (the dying mother of the baby who later turns out to be Buck Thorpe) mentioned in only three paragraphs of the original story. Once again, Foote's desire to highlight family relationships manifests itself.

Foote remembers, it was "the character of the woman [that] became alive to me, even though Faulkner gives only a few paragraphs to her" (Tomorrow: The Genesis of a Screenplay" 149-150). "I called this woman Sarah, although Faulkner never names her, and I had her married to a man named Eubanks" (153), Foote continues, relating his detailed development of the woman and her relationship to Fentry, admitting his realization that "what I had written was monstrously out of proportion to the rest of the story" (154). Once again, Foote's interest in character and his desire to sketch each one fully and compassionately arises in his adaptation of *Tomorrow*.

Foote has always taken seriously his responsibility to maintain the spirit of the original work he is adapting, so his rewriting of "Tomorrow" presented him with "a worrisome problem." He explains, "The more completely I dramatized the relationship between Fentry and Sarah, the less room it left for the dramatizing of the other elements of the story" (Tomorrow: The Genesis of a Screenplay" 157). Even stronger than his determination to deal honestly with each job, however, is the need to satisfy the inner voice that requires he be true to his philosophy; therefore, Foote felt justified in what he had done with Faulkner's characters.

Under Foote's rewriting, the detective story practically vanishes, but the love story is allowed to blossom, as Fentry acts out his growing love for the vagrant woman he finds outside his boarding house and her child that is not his. As he attempts to nurse the woman back to health, he gives her every consideration and even plans to build her the house she has always wanted. Foote allows this woman to be a "talker" like the one he created in "Old Man," and the quiet Fentry listens as she tells about her estranged family and her hopes for her unborn child, underscoring the importance of family that seems to be necessary to Foote's work.

According to Foote's version, Sarah has not only been abandoned by her husband who "just disappeared three months ago when he heard about the baby coming" (11), but she has also been rejected from her father's house. When Fentry asks if she can return to her father and brothers, she makes it clear that neither she nor her family is interested in maintaining relationships: "They asked me to leave and never come back when I married my husband, and I don't ever intend to go back," she replies firmly.

Her empirical knowledge of unfeeling family relationships restricts her initially from trusting Fentry or accepting his overtures of kindness. Fentry, who has a rather strange but personable relationship with his own father, is undaunted by her reserve or her past. The contrast between the two characters is interesting in light of the impact a father's relationship with his child can have. Sarah, who has been rejected by her father, has developed into a suspicious and somewhat unfeeling adult, while Fentry, who has enjoyed a close connection with his father, is more inclined to understand love and acceptance, even in his backward way. He offers this security to Sarah, hoping to overcome her bitter past while fulfilling his own desire to be a husband and father. Sarah's death, unfortunately, quickly follows their hasty marriage, but Fentry is determined to keep his commitment to raise her child "like he was my own" (83). He voices this dedication to the baby: "Son, your mama is dead. But I'm gonna raise you and see to you. I'll be your Papa and your Mama. And you'll never want or do without while I have breath left in my bones" (88).

Although the child is the offspring of a man who rejected it, Fentry's commitment to his "son" is strong, demonstrating Foote's understanding that it is love, rather than blood, that creates the tie between parents and their children. The film fleshes out Faulkner's scant description of the relationship between the child as he grows and his "father" in a series of silent scenes which solidify the bond between the two. This focus on Fentry and his "son" affirms the connection with the father-son theme of Foote's own plays.

When Bruce Kawin finds it "unfortunate that the relationship between Fentry and his 'son' is so hurriedly summarized" (65), he overlooks the poignant message about the father-son bond so deeply etched in Foote's montage, which Barbera calls a "delight of the film" (194).[5] For although more time is spent on Fentry and Sarah in the movie than on Fentry and the boy he names Jackson and Longstreet, most critics agree that the love of the "father" and the "son" is the more explicitly developed relationship (Yellin and Connors 12). The credit goes to Foote for following his natural tendency to highlight the father-son motif.

Fentry brings the child back to his own father's home, thereby strengthening the quiet image of Fentry's homelife as his father assures him that "if he's yours, he's welcome" (26). Still, he is unable to maintain the unit the three generations of men attempt to create: not being "flesh and blood kin," the Thorpes are able to legally and forcefully take Jackson and Longstreet to rear him as Buck Thorpe. Fentry's true role as father to his "son" and his "capacity for love" (Foote, *Tomorrow*, 159) is the more lasting, though; fifteen years later, when Fentry "can't vote Bookwright free," it is because "there still remained . . . at least the memory of that little boy . . . even though the man the boy had become didn't know it and only Fentry did" (Faulkner, "Tomorrow" 51-52).

One cannot help speculating that had Fentry retained control over Jackson and Longstreet, his loving influence on the boy almost certainly would have kept him from becoming a criminal and allowed that hope of family to become a reality for both men. This hope for the future, nurtured by the selfless love of a man for his son, is what "endures . . . tomorrow and tomorrow and tomorrow," in both Faulkner's and Foote's works. For although the ending of the film is no more uplifting than Faulkner's story, the memory of the love between the father-figure and the son that has endured for so long continues to offer at least the desire for reunion and reconciliation.

Although co-producer Paul Roebling disagreed with Foote's interpretation of "what Mr. Faulkner wrote and . . . what I wanted to put on the screen" (Yellin and Connors 171), director Joseph Anthony felt that what Foote had written was "that which was truly relevant to the basic story" (178). Robert Duvall, who insists his role as Fentry in the film is still his favorite part, applauds Foote's rewriting: "I didn't read [the Faulkner story] until after I made the movie. Horton had put in much of his own material and it was great. He knows the area and the people" (173).

Foote admits that Faulkner's story "is separate and equal and powerful," but that his own film version seems to be "the most complete, on its own, as an experience" (165). Realizing that when adapting, "there is the selfish moment [in which you] remember it is not yours, but you take it over" (Personal communication 11/14/87), Foote maintains that "I wouldn't have known how to do 'Tomorrow' except the way that I did it, and although I'm not close in form, I feel I'm close in essence to Faulkner's story" (Yellin and Connors 21).

Faulkner must have agreed, for Foote says that he was so pleased with both the television and screen renditions that he insisted Foote share the copyright with him (Personal communication 11/14/87). Many critics agree that Foote's "Tomorrow" is "one of the best screen adaptations of a Faulkner work" (Millichap 104), and Bruce Kawin calls it "simply one of the best independent productions in the recent history of American narrative film" (65). It also continues the strong thread of father-son relationships that is woven so vitally into Foote's life work.

As with "Old Man," very little has been said concerning Foote's final (to date) Faulkner adaptation, "Barn Burning," which he wrote for the PBS American Short Story Series in

1980. According to Merrill Maquire Skaggs (wife of the film's producer Calvin Skaggs), the production company and academic advisors "determined from the beginning to keep the film as faithful as possible to William Faulkner's plot" (6). No commitment was made to maintaining Faulkner's characters as written, though, and this may be a critical issue in comparing the two versions of "Barn Burning," as further discussion will demonstrate.

The story shows firebrand Abner Snopes and the family he subjects to his incendiary habit through the eyes of his son Sarty, whose desperate pride in his father finally incinerates at the end of the story when the father's lawlessness against the de Spains cannot be justified. An analysis of the two works proves this fidelity to plot was achieved, even though Skaggs intimates that Faulkner's and Foote's works do not tell the same story.

"While Faulkner's prose version is clearly about Sarty Snopes's struggle to forge an acceptable identity for himself," Skaggs writes, "the film with the same plot is clearly about something else." She goes on to assert that "the film belongs to Ab Snopes, the father," rather than to the boy, reasoning that Tommy Lee Jones, who plays Ab Snopes, "steals the show because he has the most talent to begin with" (8). Skaggs also assumes that the story belongs to the father because he totally controls his family. "He holds the reins," (11), she states. "Further, it is Abner who most often delivers the lines which *explain* the actions" (12).

While performance certainly plays an important role in determining an audience's interest in a film's characters, Skaggs' thesis is irrelevant to what either writer was attempting with the story. Both Faulkner and Foote write equally of a father *and* son relationship, in which the confused son is bullied by a father who is ferociously convinced "in the rightness of his own actions" (Faulkner, "Barn Burning" 1495). But the point of both writers can be summed up in the conflict of "blood" Snopes speaks of after his initial legal hearing when he reprimands his son for "fixing to tell them [the truth concerning the fires]" (1496). "'You've got to learn,'" he tells his son, "'You got to learn to stick to your own blood or you ain't going to have any blood to stick to you'" (1496). Sarty understands this conflict between "us" and "them" in simpler terms: "our enemy . . . ourn! Mine and hisn both! He's my father" (1493).

But the conflict cannot remain that simple. "With a surge of peace and joy," Faulkner tells us, Sarty hopes the de Spains, who seem protected in their home as "big as a courthouse," "are safe from him" and that "maybe it will change him [his father] now from what maybe he couldn't help but be" (1497-1498). Later, however, when he realizes that his father does not intend even to warn de Spain before he burns the barn, "the old blood which he had not been permitted to choose for himself, which had been bequeathed him willy nilly and which had run for so long" (1504), demands Sarty choose between the inscrutable and no longer defendable father, the "us," and the family of man of which he is also a son. Finally, Sarty grasps that blood may be thicker than water, but it cannot be thicker than truth. When the father's example can no longer be followed—symbolically not unlike Snopes' foot tracks he tried to wash from the de Spain rug—Sarty runs to the "other side," first to warn them of his father's intentions and then to strike out on his own, forging a new way of life for himself. At the end of the story, Faulkner tells us "He did not look back" (1507).

This conflict of "blood" is retained explicitly in Foote's script. In Foote's "Barn Burning," Sarty goes from acquiescing to his father's instruction that "Blood's blood. You can't change it. . . . He's right—we've got to stick or else we're nothing and we got no one" to denying that blood's power over him to keep him from doing the right thing in warning the de Spains. Many of Foote's own characters have struggled with this conflict between kin and community, and it is common in Foote's work for the larger family to win out, suggesting that one's responsibility to "love thy neighbor" is of greater value than maintaining a closed family unit. But the important difference between the two versions of "Barn Burning" occurs in the endings.

What happens to Ab Snopes in Faulkner's story? When Sarty hears shots fired and he cries, "Pap! Pap!" and later

"Father! Father!" (1506), and when he thinks of his father thereafter in the past tense: "My father... he *was* brave!... He *was*! He was in the war! He was in Colonel Sartoris' cav'ry!" (1507, my emphasis), it is easy to assume Snopes is dead. Therefore, it seems the half-orphaned Sarty has no choice in the end when he leaves, not looking back. It should be considered that he is running away from his family, having been responsible for his own father's death.

Skaggs accepts without question this interpretation of the ending, intimating that the "epic force his father represented" has been killed when Sarty leaves and "does not look back" (14). She goes on to criticize the film for depicting Sarty's abandonment of that force, because Foote does not give in to the ready assumption that the shots fired were from an unmentioned de Spain gun or that they actually killed Ab Snopes. Faulkner gives no positive conclusion and the boy's past tense speech about his father may be interpreted that his father *was* a brave man at one time (Sarty does not know that his father's activity in the army was purely mercenary) though this night's actions finally prove to Sarty that he is no longer courageous. Snopes is *metaphorically* dead and the old blood of the father can no longer "stick" to the son when the actions of the father can no longer be defended. In this sense, Sarty is not unlike John Turner Davis in Foote's earlier play when he chooses the Whytes over his aunt and uncle who have deserted him.

When the film shows Snopes leaving with his family (minus Sarty) in the wagon silhouetted against the fire, and Sarty turning to run in the opposite direction, the boy's choosing against his father in favor of the larger family of man which de Spain represents is obvious. Foote further explains Sarty's choice by letting the boy overhear earlier a discussion in town in which the truth about his father's war record is revealed: that he was a deserter and a thief and that his "war" wounds were actually the result of dealing in stolen horses. In the screenplay, Sarty is thus allowed to make a more informed decision, and the loss of his naivete about his father is spotlighted as a theme of the film.

That Foote should retain Faulkner's conflict yet clarify the boy's decision is to be expected. Although most of his own plays are concerned with the immediate family relationships, the definition of family is expanded to embrace the larger family of community and one's responsibility to humanity in nearly every script from the better known *To Kill a Mockingbird* and *Tender Mercies* to the lesser known *John Turner Davis*. The early plays, as well as the latter *Orphans' Home* cycle, also bear out this acknowledgement of the larger "community-family."

Foote himself has expressed displeasure in his own ending to the script, admitting that "Barn Burning" was hard to adapt "due to the interior monologue of the last page. The film's end was lame and didn't stand up to Faulkner's at all," he laments (Personal communication 11/14/87). While the mystery and poignancy of Faulkner's ending certainly are diminished, Foote is too hard on himself for making explicit what Faulkner merely implied. The decision Foote has Sarty make is more complex than the one Faulkner wrote for the boy, especially if Faulkner intended Snopes' death and Sarty's knowledge of it; therefore, Foote's focus on this choice seems the stronger interpretation of Faulkner's ending; either way, the change in perspective and motivation is indicative of Foote's shaping of the work. While both Faulkner's and Foote's works focus on the father-son relationship, Foote's rendition examines more deeply the impact a father's negative influence can have on a sensitive, deep-thinking son who must choose between "blood," with all its prejudice, and the larger community family. It underscores the universal point Foote's work makes, even when dealing with the personal family portrait.

Foote has commented that there comes a time in adapting someone else's work when fidelity to the original is put aside and one's own chemistry takes over. However, as Yellin and Connors have discovered, it is this chemistry that Foote and Faulkner share (21). When Foote defines a theme of his work as the deep belief in the human spirit (CBY 147), one remembers Faulkner's description of his own art as a "life's work in the agony and sweat of the human spirit" (Faulkner, "Address . . ." 723). When Foote points out that he is "attracted to the sense of dignity in the human spirit that allows [people] with grace to meet what comes their way and find strength to survive" (Neff 30), one cannot help hearing the echoes of Faulkner's Nobel Prize acceptance speech: "I believe that man will not merely endure; he will prevail . . . because he has a soul, a spirit capable of compassion and sacrifice and endurance" (724).

When David Sterritt describes Foote's style as "the thrill of watching characters grow, personalities deepen, relationships ripen and mature" (36), he aptly sums up the footprints this screenwriter has left on the novelist's legacy. More important, however, as Foote implied earlier, though the forms of their work may differ, the essence remains the same. In this marriage of minds, Foote and Faulkner speak with the same "poet's voice" (Faulkner, "Address . . .," 724).

Part II
Climbing into Another Writer's Skin:
Adapting *To Kill a Mockingbird*

Foote has learned that a writer has to "be sure he has a certain kinship with what he's adapting [because] you're trying to get under the skin of a person" (Hachem 41). It surely is no coincidence that Foote's words echo those of Harper Lee's famous lawyer-character Atticus Finch who advises his children in *To Kill a Mockingbird* that, "You never really understand a person until you consider things from his point of view . . . until you climb into his skin and walk around in it" (Lee 36). Apparently Foote came to recognize that "certain kinship" with the world of Lee's novel and his attempt to get "under her skin," so to speak, was a success, as his translation of her novel to the screen won both the 1962 Best Screenplay Oscar and the Writer's Guild Award.[6]

At first, when producer Alan J. Pakula approached Foote with Harper Lee's Pulitzer-prize-winning novel, Foote was disinclined even to read the best seller. He recalls his reluctance was due in part to the failure of *Storm Fear*, in spite of pleasant experiences with the first two Faulkner works. He was not interested in dramatizing, either, as he longed to have time for his own work. Foote's wife, though, impressed by Lee's novel, was eager to engage her husband in the project; she convinced him to consider the offer further.

Foote was still reluctant to make a commitment; he complained to Pakula that "it would be a back-breaking job because it [the novel] sprawls all over." The producer assured him there was room for different approaches since Lee herself had been offered the adaptation opportunity but was not interested. "You are her first choice and our first choice," Pakula persuaded. Foote, completely charmed by Lee when they met, credits the author with winning him over to the assignment: "I just loved her . . . And I thought, 'Well, I'll enjoy this, if no more than getting to know her'" (Barr 149).

Foote's own Southern heritage and memories of "tree houses, small towns, black cooks, and people like Boo Radley" that make up Lee's fictionalized milieu enabled him finally to arrive at the place where he forgot that she had written it and thought of *To Kill a Mockingbird* as his own (Personal communication 11/14/87). But perhaps what really attracted Foote to the world Lee had created (or recreated from her personal experience) and made him feel at home there was his identification with the portrayal of a father and his children and the development of the father-child theme so prevalent in his own work.

Adapting is "an enormous responsibility toward somebody's work," Foote instructs, "and I don't believe that you should take the work you're adapting as a departure to do something else" (Hachem 41). Facing the necessity of cutting the story's two-year span to align with budget and running-time requirements, Foote was forced to condense the material to two summers and two months of the following autumns. However, as Lee's rather loosely winding narrative somewhat slows down the novel, Foote's tightening is an improvement rather than a deliberate departure.

Barr points out that this compression of time and events can "run the risk of becoming too abrupt." He criticizes, "at times, scenes may appear unmotivated, while the characters may be reduced to one-dimensional stereotypes" (150). However, Foote's reduction of many of the novel's scenes and characters allows for the focus on the family theme to which Foote returns in most, if not all, of his work, original or otherwise. It also allows the major roles more time to develop and for Foote to demonstrate his careful construction of each character.

Through his homing in to this single message, one can observe more plainly the emphasis on the father-child relationships that are an important part of Lee's novel but are obscured there by accompanying detail. These relationships include those of Atticus and his children, Jem and Scout; Dill and his "fathers"; the Cunninghams; Bob and Mayella Ewell; Boo Radley and his father, as well as his identification with the Finch children as "his own." They are brought to the forefront of the film, even taking the spotlight from the admittedly fascinating rape trial and the mystery of Boo Radley. Foote's "kinship" with this theme, as demonstrated in the rest of his work, allows him to highlight it even more than the novel was capable of doing. It is Foote's familiar signature and allows him to consider the work his own.

The screenplay therefore deletes Maycomb's historical background, and the Finch family history, cutting out extended family members and family reunions detailed in the novel. While these flesh out the family theme, they merely cloud the focus on the immediate family relationship between Atticus and his children. Both Aunt Alexandra's visit and Atticus' stint with the state legislature are omitted, as they detract from Atticus' role as both father and mother to his children.

The chapter on Mrs. Dubose's attempt to overcome a morphine addiction has no connection with other parts of the story and is reduced to a single, short scene in the movie which serves to demonstrate Atticus' graciousness rather than the old lady's courage. Again Foote focuses attention on the father and dismisses anything that might confuse that issue. Other details, including minor characters such as the Misses Tutti and Frutti, Mr. Dolphus Raymond, Mr. Link Deas, Mr. Avery, Mr. Underwood, and Mr. X. Billups have to be overlooked for the sake of time; they also have no role in enhancing Foote's focus on the father-child theme.

Calpurnia (Cal), the Finches' black cook, is just as lovingly sketched in the screenplay as in the book, and Foote's care and respect for Southern black characters is in complete sympathy with Lee's own concern. Cal is the only character whose role as a substitute mother even slightly rivals Atticus' role; Foote does not reduce her to the Hollywood "mammy" stereotype, but he does not call excessive attention to her at the expense of the other main characters.

One may regret Foote's cutting the first-grade classroom scenes for their comic value, but as they serve no purpose in the development of his theme, they are reduced to Scout's report of the events to Atticus, allowing his instruction to her concerning the situation to be spotlighted instead. Foote creates another scene introducing Scout's first day of school, when he shows the whole Finch family, complete with Cal and Miss Maudie, too, at the breakfast table; before Scout rushes off to school with Jem, she makes a point of kissing her father goodbye. The Scout of Lee's novel probably would not allow for such sentiment, but Foote's character is more softly drawn, especially in relation to her love for her father. In fact, all the characters' "edges," made sharp by Scout's somewhat sarcastic narration in the novel, are rounded off in Foote's adaptation, further evidence of Foote's charitable style.

The screenplay sketches out more fully the role of the widowed Atticus as both father and mother. Before going to sleep, Scout asks to see her father's watch and recites the inscription on the back: "To Atticus, my beloved husband." She goes on to relate that Jem has claimed the watch will "belong to him someday," and Atticus agrees that it is "customary for the boy to have his father's watch." It is important to Foote that the traditional father-son relationship be alluded to here, as well as the typical mother-daughter heritage, for when Scout asks what she will have, her father remembers there are some pieces of her mother's jewelry that will be hers.

This conversation instigates Scout's thinking somewhat wistfully about the mother she never knew, as Mrs. Finch died when Scout was only two years old; Jem, who remembers their mother, supplies the missing details. During this exchange, the camera focuses on Atticus sitting alone on the porch listening pensively to his children's talk of their deceased mother, his absent wife. It is Foote's intention to spotlight Atticus as a survivor, overcoming his own heartbreak to be both mother and father for his children.

There seems to be little or no awareness of Atticus' loneliness in the novel; one paragraph in the book sums up the deceased mother, neatly and even coldly. Scout flatly admits in the book, "I did not miss her," and only Jem is shown to reflect on his loss occasionally. Foote knowingly adds these details, filling out the characters with more human tenderness. These are obvious "Foote" touches on a family portrait, as in all his work he finds significant the development of the family unit, complete with its traditions and emotions.

Terry Barr asserts that "in many ways, Lee's Atticus Finch is Horton Foote's kind of character: the head of a broken family; a relentless dreamer and believer in the basic honor and dignity of all living creatures, [who is] also a reluctant realist" (152-153). Indeed, he fits the cast of characters that people so much of Foote's original work which is based on people from Foote's own past. Barr continues: "undoubtedly, one of the chief factors that endeared Foote to the work was its treatment of Jem and Scout, who had no mother to nurture them, but who had a father who, if any person could, successfully filled the role of both parents." Many of Foote's plays portray families in which one parent attempts to handle both parental roles, though usually not as adequately as Atticus who exemplifies Foote's ideal parent.

Foote admits that these scenes outlined above are drawn from memories of his own past in which he "used to lie in bed at night and listen to the grown-ups talking outside" (Barr 157). In another interview he explained: "I took the characters and put them in different situations. Like that scene when the children are in their bedrooms and they can hear them talking . . . That's me listening to my mother" (Wood, LFQ 229).

In relation to his family focus, Foote understands the importance of Scout's altercation with Walter Cunningham in the schoolyard; therefore he uses it to pinpoint other father relationships. Because the impoverished Cunninghams are proud, the only way Jem can convince Walter to join them at their house for the noon meal is to remind him that "our daddy's a friend of your daddy's" (44). Indeed, the opening scene of the film portrays the business-related friendship between the two fathers, Mr. Finch and Mr. Cunningham, different as their lifestyles may be.

Establishing a friendship between fathers is important even to children and serves as impetus enough for Walter to join them for the first nourishing dinner he has had in a long time. He aggravates Jem's resentment at Atticus, however, for not being allowed to own a gun when Walter admits that he has had one for "a year or so" and that he and his father "go hunting in our spare time" (45). In spite of the poverty in which the Cunninghams are forced to live, there is no evidence that Mr. Cunningham is a poor father to his children; Walter's exchange here demonstrates the opposite, and even more specifically than Lee describes in the novel. Foote's care in establishing his characters fully and with understanding is exhibited in the development of the Cunninghams. Ignoring most of the demeaning descriptions of that family in the novel, Foote chooses to accentuate the positive characteristics.

Scout's childhood courtship with Dill Harris is greatly tightened from the book, and most of Dill's background is summarized in a few, well-chosen words about his own family experience. Harper Lee suggested Foote recall Truman Capote on whom her character is based in order to visualize the character, but as Foote did not know Capote, he had to invent "a lot of Dill" (Wood, LFQ 229). Dill makes his first appearance early in the film, and when Jem expresses doubts about Dill's age—"You look right puny for goin' on seven"—Dill responds, "I'm little, but I'm old." It does not take long for the audience to come to an understanding about Dill's "seven-going-on-seventeen" facade: he has obviously had to rear himself, as his parents have little time for him.

The opening exchange when the children first meet Dill allows Foote's focus on the importance of fathers to shine through. Scout informs Dill, "Our mama's dead, but we got a daddy," indicating her view that it hardly matters if one's mother is dead, when one has a father as caring as Atticus. She is confused to learn Dill does not have a father, even though he is not dead, and in the time-lapse that her confusion causes, Dill creates his fantasy father: "My daddy owns the L and N Railroad. He's going to let me run the engine all the way to New Orleans" (11). After he knows the Finches better, Dill informs them that his "daddy was a railroad man 'til he got rich. Now he flies airplanes," he brags. "One of these days he's just goin' to swoop down here to Maycomb, pick me up, and take me for a ride" (67). Dill spends a large amount of his time separated from his indifferent mother and stepfather; this, and his pathetic need to fabricate a loving father for himself, brings into sharp relief the near-perfect relationship Atticus has with his children.

The novel includes a scene where Dill runs away from home to live with the Finches because he knows he is not wanted by his own family. When Scout, who is naive about a neglect which contrasts sharply with her own family security, tries to convince Dill that his family cannot do without him, Dill sets her misconceptions straight by explaining his parents' impatient approach: "They buy me everything I want, but it's now-you've-got-it-go-play-with-it" (154). Though Foote cut this dialogue from the screenplay, the mere lingering of the camera in one scene of the film on the lonely child's wistful face as his friends leave him alone outside to go inside their house with their father truly covers a multitude of details from the book. While this may be explained as the advantage of the camera over the printed page, the scene is clearly in line with everything else Foote has chosen from Lee's narrative to enhance his theme.

The obsession Jem, Scout, and Dill have with the Boo Radley mystery which meanders throughout the entire novel is neatly summed up in a few tight scenes in the screenplay that detail the sordid background from the book. But while Lee allows the children's morbid curiosity about their unfortunate neighbor to ramble throughout her narrative, Foote cuts through the sensationalism of local gossip about Boo, alluding to it only briefly, to the sentiment closer to his heart: Boo and his desire for a happy family relationship. Rather than exploit the local legends enumerated in the novel about the character, Foote allows for a more human and sympathetic Boo to fill the screen.

Foote further develops Boo's shy attempts at friendship with Jem and Scout already present in Lee's book by clearing away the debris of unrelated detail to highlight the significant: his gifts of the soap dolls and other odd items placed in the hollow of a tree near both their houses; his mending of Jem's pants, torn in the children's unredeeming late-night escapade to "get a look" at their "monster-neighbor"; and his risking his life and committing murder to save the children when Bob Ewell cowardly attacks Jem and Scout to get even with their father.

That Arthur Radley and his own father do not have a loving relationship is brought out briefly, but explicitly as Jem tries to explain the phenomenon of Boo Radley to newcomer Dill. When Boo's father Mr. Radley passes their yard, Jem points him out to Dill as "the meanest man that ever took a breath of life," elaborating: "he has a boy named Boo that he keeps chained to a bed in that house over yonder" (12). To Jem, and to both Lee and Foote, the crime of mistreating one's children is the cruelest anyone could commit.

As Jem continues his description of their larger-than-life neighbor, Dill's Aunt Stephanie joins the conversation.[7] She dutifully follows Jem's directive to "tell about the time Boo tried to kill his papa," describing how Boo supposedly stabbed his father in the leg with the scissors. "They wanted to send him to an asylum," Aunt Stephanie concludes, "but his daddy said no Radley was going to any asylum. So they locked him up in the basement of the Courthouse till he nearly died of the damp, and his daddy brought him home" (14).

The motivation behind Boo's alleged attack on his father, at the age of 33, is not outlined clearly by either author, but in both the book and the screenplay Mr. Radley is more interested in the family reputation than the family's well-being. In the novel, Lee hints at the suspected child abuse to which Boo may have been subjected, and while Foote leaves out such descriptions in the screenplay, perhaps to keep from completely vilifying Boo's father, he does call attention to Mr. Radley's sealing up the hole in the oak tree where Boo has hidden his treasures for Jem and Scout to find. In the novel, it is Mr.

Nathan Radley, Boo's brother, who puts cement into the knothole, a hateful and selfishly motivated act. Lee explains that after Boo's father died, his brother Mr. Nathan "took Mr. Radley's place. The only difference between him and his father was their ages" (19).

Mr. Nathan Radley is not mentioned in Foote's screenplay, probably in an effort to reduce the number of characters of which the audience has to keep track. Foote's story suggests that it is solely the father who prevents his son's attempt at making friends. Foote combines the two Mr. Radleys, too, so as to not confuse the issue of the father's possible abusive conduct with Boo, putting an emphasis on father-son relationships, rather than on the sibling rivalry that may have existed between Arthur and his brother Nathan. Foote accentuates the insight into Boo's background to elicit the audience's sympathy for the character and to make his lifestyle easier for the audience to comprehend, rather than creating a monster-figure to fulfill the audience's Hollywood expectations.

Perhaps it is the longing for loving family ties that incites Boo to keep a watchful, caring eye on the Finch children—"his children," in Lee's words. Summing up the story as seen from Boo's eyes, the final pages of the novel voice this perspective better than the film which omits the following lines:

> It was summertime, and two children scampered down the sidewalk toward a man approaching in the distance. . . . [and] played in the front yard with their friend . . . It was fall, and his children . . . trotted to and fro around the corner, the day's woes and triumphs on their faces. They stopped at an oak tree, delighted, puzzled, apprehensive. . . . Summer and he watched his children's heart break. Autumn again, and Boo's children needed him (293-294).

Watching the two children he has grown to love give their affection to their real father, even while they act out misconceived notions about Boo himself, Boo does not hesitate when the opportunity arises for him to demonstrate his concern for them. In a strange way, his actions on their behalf may atone for the lack of love he has known from his own family. And in her limited way, Scout senses this need for affection when she assures Boo, after he has saved them from Bob Ewell's attack, that he can "pet" Jem, if only while he is asleep.

Neither Foote nor Barr credits the film's ending with sustaining that of the novel. Barr writes, "Foote's ending . . . simply does not carry the weight that Lee's ending does. . . . The omission of this further delineation of Scout's understanding sharply distinguishes the novel from the film and clearly shows the problems of adapting one work to another" (160). It may be true that a large portion of the film's audience may miss the subtlties of Boo's feelings for the Finch children in the few words the screenplay gives Scout at the end: "Boo was our neighbor. He gave us two soap dolls, a broken watch and chain, a knife, and our lives," though she goes on to demonstrate her understanding when she concludes, "Atticus said you never really knew a man until you stood in his shoes and walked around in them. Just standin' on the Radley porch was enough" (116). These lines from the film bring the focus back to what she has learned from her father, again shifting the emphasis to Foote's theme.

As far as the father-child relationship between Atticus and Scout is concerned, the film's closing lines are equal to the novel's as they both bring the spotlight back to shine on Atticus' love for his children. Both the novel and the screenplay depict Atticus' all-night vigil over his injured son, and Scout's voice assures us that "he would be there [in Jem's room] all night, and he would be there when Jem waked up in the morning" (296/117). For it is the father-child relationship between Atticus and his son and daughter that both Lee and Foote want highlighted. Harper Lee was delighted with Foote's rendition of her lifework; in a foreword to the published film script, she wrote:

> The complaints of novelists whose work has been transferred to screen are so numerous and so often justified that I sometimes wonder if I am a minority of one when I examine my own feeling about the film, *To Kill a Mockingbird*. So often one hears that . . . the novelist's own view of life is not fulfilled on the screen. . . . For me, Maycomb is there, its people are there: in two short hours one lives a childhood and lives it with Atticus Finch, whose view of life was the heart of the novel (v).

The opening scene of the film goes right to the heart of the novel and the theme Foote also wants to get across, as it quickly moves in to focus on the family home of Atticus Finch and his children. At first, six-year-old Scout appears to have an appreciation for her father that is not shared by her ten-year-old brother. Jem, pouting because his father refuses to play football, complains, "Every time I want him to do something . . . he's too old" (9). He is unimpressed when Atticus reminds him, "after all, I'm the only father you have" (7).

Perhaps Lee sums it up best in the novel when she writes, "Atticus was feeble: he was nearly 50. . . . and there was nothing Jem or I could say about him when our classmates said, 'My father—'" (97). Therefore, it becomes important to both writers that the children become convinced of their father's worth. Foote extracts these vital scenes from the novel, giving them significance in his screenplay.

Because much of Foote's intentions in the screenplay can be understood from what he omits from the novel, the same can be said about what he chooses to include. The incident with Tim Johnson, the rabid dog, has nothing whatsoever to do with the more spectacular focus on Tom Robinson or Boo Radley, but Foote leaves the dog scene in his script, because it characterizes what he considers the more important theme, the relationship between fathers and their children and how they come to love and respect one another.

When Sheriff Tate insists that Atticus shoot the rabid dog, the children protest ignorantly; when Atticus brings the dog down with one shot, Foote writes, "Jem and Scout are dumfounded. . . . The children approach Atticus reverently." Jem's speechless admiration for his father leads Tate to tease, "What's the matter, boy? Can't you talk? Didn't you know your daddy's the best shot in this county?" (54) For the first time, Jem sees his father through eyes unblinded by youth or childish prejudice. Thereafter, he knows he can count on this man for truly important things, and Jem wants his father to know that Atticus can count on him when necessary.

The real test of a father's influence comes when his children respond positively to his teaching. Foote develops a scene from the novel to illustrate this point so vital to his perception of the ideal parent-child relationship. When Atticus accepts the criminal case for Tom Robinson, the black man accused of raping Mayella Ewell, his name and the term "nigger-lover" become synonymous in Maycomb. To ease the resulting pain and confusion his children naturally experience, Atticus tries to explain why he is defending a black man against the prejudices of the community. "If I didn't," he tells Scout as he hugs her close, "I couldn't hold my head up in this town. I couldn't even tell you and Jem not to do somethin' again" (61/83).

Even though the family may experience difficulty during this period, Atticus realizes he must stand by his principles if he is ever to be a role-model for his children. And hard as it may be for them, he understands the need for his young children to develop a mature attitude if they are to survive the situation and grow up equipped to battle the prejudices from which they are suffering now. For this reason, he makes Scout promise she will not fight anyone who calls Atticus a "nigger-lover."

Scout's desire to keep this promise made to her father is the only thing that keeps her from fighting her father's critics. Lee has Scout explain, "Atticus so rarely asked Jem and me to do something for him, I could take being called a coward for him" (84-85). The maturity the young Scout shows here reflects her appreciation of the relationship she and her parent enjoy, as well as her limited understanding of her father's values.

Jem's chance to display his deepening commitment to his father comes when Atticus is forced to sit guard at the jail where Tom Robinson awaits his trial, lest anyone attempt a lynching. The children venture out in the night to keep a watch on their father, just as the lynch mob shows up. Afraid of what might occur, Atticus orders the children to go home, but for the first time, Jem refuses to do as his father demands. Foote describes the scene: "Jem shakes his head 'no.' Atticus' fists go to his hips and so do Jem's, and they face each other in defiance" (73).

Jem's concern for his father's safety drives him to disobey his father for the first time in his life. This confrontation between parent and child, brought on by their concern for each other, is not an uncommon situation in many of Foote's plays and indicates how the father has influenced his child's maturity. What makes this scene special, though, is that Jem's rebellion clearly is motivated by his love for his father, rather than his desire to run his own life, as is the case with most of Foote's characters who take stands against their parents. The relationship between Jem and Atticus is a rare one, and Foote holds it up as the ideal.

Scout saves the evening from becoming violent when she calls attention to Mr. Cunningham whom she recognizes in the crowd. Her request that he say hello to his son for her also serves as a reminder to Mr. Cunningham that he is a father, too; embarrassed, Mr. Cunningham changes mind about his intentions with the mob that evening and suggests his true character as a good father when Foote has him say, "I'll tell Walter you said 'hey,' little lady. Let's clear outta here. Let's go, boys" (75).

Establishing a relationship between the fathers helped create a friendship between Walter and the Finch children in the earlier dinner scene; in this scene the relationship between the children keeps the fathers from breaking their own understanding of what it means to be good neighbors. The impact Atticus's life and the values he has tried to teach his children have had their desired effect, both on his children and on the community, as Scout, in this particular incident, acts out her father's convictions. She and Jem demonstrate the legacy they have inherited from their father's example and their love for him in this scene more explicitly than anywhere else in either novel or film.

To establish Atticus as the "perfect" father-figure, both Lee and Foote employ other characters for comparison. The father held in sharpest contrast to Atticus is Bob Ewell, the parent of the alleged rape victim. Lee describes the white-trash Ewell family as filthy, ignorant, and mean; and the father of this family as "a man [who] spends his relief checks on green whiskey [while] his children [cry] from hunger pains" (37). Even first-graders know the problems of the Ewell family: "Ain't got no mother and their paw's right contentious" (33), one little boy explains to the new teacher. In the adaptation, Foote, again, omits much of Lee's derogatory description of the Ewell family in his usual generous manner;

however, Foote can do little to clean up a character as despicable as Bob Ewell.

Bob Ewell's realization that Atticus actually plans to defend Tom Robinson leads to his threatening the lawyer. Foote has him spit out at Atticus, both literally and figuratively, "What kind of man are you? You got chillun of your own" (31), an adequate foreshadowing for the climax of the film where Bob Ewell demonstrates the kind of man he is by attempting to murder Atticus' children, too much the coward to approach the man himself. His threat is especially hypocritical in light of how he treats his own family. When he later testifies at the Robinson trial, he reveals the lack of concern he had for the "mighty beat up" condition in which he most likely had placed his daughter on the evening of "the night in question" (which Foote changes from November to August 21).

Mayella, in spite of her calculated and rehearsed attempt to say nothing negative about her father for fear he might punish her, is the strongest witness against him at the trial, as she unwittingly exposes his abusive nature in her testimony. Obviously "the victim of cruel poverty and ignorance" (97), Foote's depiction of Mayella elicits the pity even of the children, but it is Tom Robinson's admitted pity for her, a black man's sympathy for a white woman, that closes the case against him. Regardless of Atticus' efforts on behalf of Tom, he is found guilty.

Foote had to summarize the trial scene for the shortened film, modifying language and its implications. Lee's description of the rape is more explicit, and she points a more accusing finger at Mayella's father for the attack. In the novel, Tom Robinson testifies that Mayella told him she had "never kissed a grown man before . . . [that] what her papa do to her don't count" (206), implying that Mayella is sexually abused by her father, as well as beaten. This is more than Foote's audience would have swallowed, or perhaps Foote himself is reluctant to allude to such atrocities. It also may be Foote's attempt to "give the devil his due," in this case, Bob Ewell, by not painting the man as evil as Lee created him to be in the novel. Foote is careful to curtail the use of the word "nigger," too, using it only when unavoidable.

The screenplay, however, only brightens the spotlight Lee puts on Atticus when, after the trial, the entire balcony of onlookers—the black section of the courtroom, where Jem and Scout also have been allowed to sit—stands in respect for this white man who had the compassion and courage to defend one of their own. And Jem and Scout's admiration for their father and comprehension of him as a man who was "born to do our unpleasant jobs for us" (102), comes into clearer focus as they, too, stand in honor of their father at the Rev. Sykes' urging: "Miss Jean Louise, stand up. Your father's passin'" (101).

No one viewing the movie can misunderstand Atticus Finch or his "view of life," which Harper Lee claims is the "heart" of both the novel and Foote's film. Even New York *Times* film critic Bosley Crowther alluded to the point both Lee and Foote attempted to make when he wrote that the "crucial" focus of the film is "the relationship between Atticus and his children" (10:2).

Harper Lee herself went on to say in her foreword to the published screenplay that:

> "Horton Foote's screenplay is a work of such quiet and unobtrusive excellence that many people have commented on the fact that the film's dialogue was lifted chapter and verse from the novel. This is simply not so. Scenes humorous, scenes tender, scenes terrifying, each with a definite purpose and value, blended so delicately with the original, created the illusion that these were Harper Lee's words. If the integrity of a film adaptation is measured by the degree to which the novelist's intent is preserved, Mr. Foote's screenplay should be studied as a classic" (v).

Lee astutely recognizes Foote's signature on her work, and her assessment of his integrity and genius is correct. While all the scenes she mentions above are suggested in her novel, Foote's re-ordering and re-writing make the screenplay as important as the original book. While the novel won the Pulitzer Prize, Foote's screenplay was awarded both the Oscar and the Writers Guild Award that year. Lee's awareness, too, of Foote's "definite purpose"—i.e., to bring to the forefront the relationship between fathers and their families, particularly Atticus and his children—is significant. It is as though Foote actually did climb into Lee's skin and walk around, but the footprints he left behind are deepened by the weight of his own interest, style, and purpose.

Lee concludes, in the foreword to the screenplay, that "perhaps *To Kill a Mockingbird* marks the beginning of a new era or responsibility in Hollywood: its producers, its screenwriter, and its actors have kept faith with a novel, for better or worse, and the result is a film that has a life of its own as a work of art" (v). With Horton Foote as screenwriter, and with an understanding director and producer, Lee's comments may very well be true. But when the three filling those important positions don't share the same vision for the work, too often the writer's words are erased in favor of bigger figures on the financial bottom line. Foote was to realize that unfortunate reality through his experience with other adaptation assignments for Hollywood.

Part III
"Getting into the Nature of Adapting": Other Adaptations for Hollywood and Television

Following the success of *To Kill a Mockingbird*, it would seem that Foote had found a niche in Hollywood where he felt at home. But, even though he had enjoyed the Harper Lee project and achieved much acclaim from his contribution, he was still anxious to continue in his own original work. "I was getting into the nature of adapting," Foote recalls, "which is very upsetting to me because I was losing my identity" (Wood, LFQ 228).

Unfortunately, neither Hollywood nor Broadway appeared to be the milieu for his value system, as the 1960's and 1970's continued in a vein with which Foote felt he had nothing in common. He was confused by the disregard for morality displayed in the worlds of film and theatre and the gluttonous commercialism of both. Caught in the midst of the race riots and the Viet Nam protest demonstrations, to Foote, the entire country seemed to be coming apart at the seams: "the drugs, the racial tensions . . . I didn't know what the hell was going on" (Barr 164), he has admitted on several occasions.

He took advantage of his confusion and disgust to escape New York for New Hampshire where he began writing the nine-play cycle based on his own father's life that he had longed to create, supporting himself and his family with small projects, including a few of the dreaded adaptations. He also found time during this period to adapt his play *The Travelling Lady* to screen.

Hurry Sundown, the next major adaptation assignment, could have resulted in a meaningful project; in fact, Foote admits he was anxious to work with producer-director Otto Preminger because of his reputation as an "old Hollywood tough" (Barr 162). Preminger apparently was just as eager to sign Foote for the job; Barr suggests that not only was Preminger banking on the popularity of Foote's recent Oscar for the screenplay of *To Kill a Mockingbird*, but also he must have felt that *Hurry Sundown*'s timely racial theme was something with which Foote would feel at home (161-162). Looking back on the assignment, Foote dismisses Preminger's motives with disdain: "Hollywood, being the copycat that it often is, any time there was a third-rate, or fourth-rate, or a fifth-rate Southern novel, they'd call me up and everyone thought I was a Southern specialist" (Edgerton 5).

Although Foote disliked K. B. Gilden's best-selling novel from which the adaptation would be taken, he agreed to create a working draft for Preminger's perusal. Unfortunately, he and Preminger could not come to terms over what Foote had already written; so he withdrew from the project. Preminger, however, insisted that Foote share credit for screen writing with Thomas Ryan, who completed the adaptation; Foote acquiesced only because he felt obligated to Preminger for paying him such a large sum. Still, Foote has refused even to view the 1966 film at its completion, unable to see how there could be anything in it of interest to him (Barr 162-163). "I am very embarrassed about [it]," he confesses. "I have never seen [it]" (Wood, LFQ 228).

Critics agree that the film was badly directed and produced (Millichap 104); but in spite of a contrived, convoluted plot with stereotypic characters and a melodramatic tone, there is something of value in the film in relation to this discussion: a focus on the bond that exists between fathers and sons. Whether or not this subject was introduced by Foote and maintained and developed by Ryan has not been ascertained, but, contrary to Barr's claim that *Hurry Sundown* bears "little resemblance to any of Foote's other work" (163), it deserves attention here in view of Foote's consistency in portraying that theme.[8]

Henry Warren, living off his wife's old Southern name (Colifax) and money, schemes to sell all her Georgia family land to an oil company in a plan (not unlike that in Foote's *Oil Well*) to go from being "land poor to money rich." Having bought and sold already all the Colifax land, he only lacks his cousin Rad's farm and that of a black family by the name of Scott. Neither of these two families can be manipulated by Henry, though, and joining together in a black-white union, unheard of in the mid-1940's, they are able to ruin his plans. Even when Henry has the local Klan dynamite the land in retaliation, the interracial connection proves stronger, and in the end, Henry loses the entire deal. Even worse, his wife throws him out of their home. Trying to sell family land for oil money, he ends up losing everything.

Enter Horton Foote and his focus on family relationships. Henry's family life is fraught with problems from the beginning. Unfaithful to his wife Julie, whom he abuses, he also has a six-year-old son Coli who suffers from an emotional disturbance caused by Henry's neglect when he was an infant. Henry is to repeat this type of neglect later in the movie, this time nearly killing his son, and when Julie discovers Henry's behavior, she quietly but firmly kicks him out of their life. That he is a man whose business is more important than his family clearly makes Henry a villain, at least from the perspective of Foote's theme concerning fathers and their children.

It is no coincidence, as far as Foote's championing human relationships over materialism goes, that Henry's impoverished cousin Rad, on the other hand, enjoys a healthy family of four children and a loving wife. The screenplay implies, though, that a father must be present to instill his values in his children; while Rad was away in the war, Henry has attempted, successfully, to replace his own estranged son with Rad's. Charles is eager to emulate Henry in everything, and when Rad goes to court to protect their land from Henry, Charles tips Henry off; when embarrassed by his father's stand against Henry in favor of the black neighbors, the child runs away to his uncle.

Rad, ignoring Charles' outburst of hatred toward him, firmly makes the boy return to his own family, saying, "I don't care what you think about me. I'm still your father and I aim to see that you do what's right." Like Atticus in *To Kill a Mockingbird*, Rad believes that his stand against the prejudiced and greedy of the community is the right example for his children, even if they do not share his conviction now; this comparison with Foote's ideal father puts Rad in a favorable light in this discussion.

Foote is careful to show all sides of a character, suggesting that few villains are all bad. Whether or not Foote developed Henry's character in *Hurry Sundown*, a more sympathetic side to Henry is exposed when he discovers Charles may be in danger of the dynamite he has just planted. Henry races out, only to find Charles running away from home again. However, when the dynamite explodes and the boy realizes that his real father may be killed, he finally understands which "father" he really loves. Breaking loose from Henry, he runs back into the explosion to find Rad. When Charles is pulled dead from the rising water around the dynamited house, his attempt at reconciliation with his father, though aborted, redeems the child, from Foote's stand point anyway. Henry at least cries for the boy, indicating some compassion and maturity on his part, though just how long-lasting his grief will be is uncertain; still, Henry's exhibition of sorrow is another indication of the fully humanized character that is Foote's style.

Rad mourns the death of his eldest son; "I killed him just as much as if I'd put a bullet through his head," he sobs, regretting that he and his son quarreled their last time together. His wife, however, comforts him with the truth: "But he was running to you not away," she reminds him. "He must have known how you really felt." They draw their remaining children to them for support in their time of grief, and their family unit, though diminished by one, is stronger than it has ever been. Whether or not this family focus is Foote's contribution to the film is unknown, but it fits neatly in the pattern established in his other work.

Hurry Sundown, for better or worse in Foote's career, is credited to his name; just how much of the final adaptation is actually Foote's cannot easily be determined, at least until Foote himself agrees to view the movie. A close study of the film intimates, however, that perhaps it is closer to Foote's philosophy than one might immediately surmise. While there is much that removes it from the Foote canon, the father-son theme is prevalent and lends itself to such examination.

The final (to date) feature film adaptation Foote agreed to was a translation to screen of Theodore V. Olsen's novel, *The Stalking Moon*, in 1969. With Robert Mulligan directing and Alan J. Pakula producing, it would seem that Foote was among friends who understood his creative approach; however, before the production was too advanced, Foote again quarreled over "suggested changes" and requested that his name be deleted from the credits. His request was granted, and Foote admits, "I have never seen *The Stalking Moon*" (Personal correspondence 7/28/89).

I have seen *The Stalking Moon*, a "western" of sorts, and I am convinced that Foote would have felt very much at home with the ultimate rendition. As much as any Foote work, the film again focuses on the bond between fathers and sons and does so with great sensitivity and dignity. Unlike *Hurry Sundown*, perhaps, there is little here to embarrass one's association with it. The credits go to Alvin Sargent, for the screenplay, and Wendell Mayes, for the adaptation.[9]

Briefly, Sam Varner is leaving his post of fifteen years as Army scout to settle down on his New Mexico farm. His Army "family," especially Nick, a young half-breed Indian scout who sees Sam as a father-figure, is reluctant to lose Sam and his expertise against the Indians in the Arizona territory. On his final Indian raid, a white woman by the name of Sarah who was captured by the Indians ten years before, is rescued. Despite all probable trouble, she insists on keeping her half-breed son and fleeing her Indian "husband," Salvaje. Sam's unconscious desire for a family surfaces, as he takes the woman and her son into his home, risking his life to protect Sarah and the boy from Salvaje, who proves his devotion to his son by tracking the family down to Sam's ranch, killing everyone in his path. During the conflict that ensues between the Indian and the white man as they battle over possession of the boy, the father-son theme unfolds its many layers.

Not only do we see the obvious love the Indian has for his son, we also see the boy's desire to be with his father, demonstrated by his trying to run away to join him every chance he gets. More and more, Sam reveals his own feeling for the boy and his mother as he nearly dies to protect them from the Indian. Nick, the half-breed scout, turns up to warn Sam of Salvaje's approach and gives his life trying to protect his "adoptive father" from Salvaje. Sam's love for his "son" Nick is illustrated poignantly when the scout dies; we see his transferring that feeling to Sarah's son when he bestows Nick's prized possession, a pack of cards, on the boy, who thereafter seems to accept Sam and his new home.

Eventually, Sam is successful in killing Salvaje and keeping his new-found family. The mounting suspense, as well as thoughtful performances, establish *The Stalking Moon* as a western of value in its genre, one I believe Foote ultimately would have been proud to claim. While it cannot be measured just how much of the final screenplay bears Foote's stamp, it is almost uncanny how much of it bears his spirit, particularly in the area of the father-son theme. Each character is thoughtfully portrayed, and even Salvaje is sketched sympathetically, as his vicious actions are the result of his desire to keep his son. These relationships suggest Foote's hand, whether he deserves the credit or not.

The next adaptation opportunity, a musical version of Margaret Mitchell's *Gone With the Wind*, was offered to Foote by Harold Fielding, a British theatre producer.[10] Foote approached the assignment with great expectations, but it was not long before Foote realized the multi-million dollar project was not going to yield anything more sound than a "soap opera" (Barr 165). After a brief run in London and Los

Angeles, the musical fell into oblivion. Chagrinned, Foote maintains his involvement with the piece was "nothing I played for keeps for" (Barr 166), even though it was a financial boon for the Foote family.

An adaptation of Flannery O'Connor's short story, "The Displaced Person," was more satisfying; Foote agreed to undertake the project in 1977 for PBS' *American Short Story Series*.[11] Again, here was the Southern milieu with which Foote could easily identify, but as it was a short story, the headaches of corralling large, sprawling works as the previous novels had been were eliminated. O'Connor's story, very much a single note lifted from the entire O'Connor symphony of modern Southern heritage, transposed neatly into the genre of film. Besides these good reasons for Foote's association with the O'Connor piece, Foote laughs, "I'm almost like one of those crazy Protestants she writes about!" (Wood, LFQ 229)

"The Displaced Person," which Foote adapted nearly verbatim from page to screen, tells the story of the widowed Mrs. McIntyre attempting to hang on to her late husband's farm. Having depended for years on shiftless tenants who inefficiently run the farm, she believes she has found her salvation in the hard-working Guizacs, a Polish family displaced from their homeland by the tortures of Nazi-Europe. Unfortunately, Mr. Guizac offends his employer's racist philosophy, and, too cowardly to fire the innocent man herself, Mrs. McIntyre allows a tragic accident she could have prevented to take the man's life. One by one every hired hand leaves the place, neglecting a now-bedridden Mrs. McIntyre. Though she is still on "her place," in the end, she is as displaced as all the rest.

The crux of the work lies in a conversation Mrs. McIntyre has with the priest before the accident occurs. Having introduced the displaced people to the widow, the priest hopes to introduce the widow to the Catholic church. She wants only to complain about the intruders the Priest has brought her, though, so he turns his attention to her beautiful peacocks. Just as Mrs. McIntyre whines that Mr. Guizac "doesn't fit in" (225), the bird spreads his stunning tail and the Priest is transfixed; "Christ will come like that!" he exclaims. Still complaining about her displaced person, though, Mrs. McIntyre insists, "He didn't have to come here in the first place." The Priest, still caught up in his epiphany, replies, "He came to redeem us" (226).

One is reminded of Mrs. McIntyre's early admission that Mr. Guizac "is my salvation" (203) against the shiftlessness of former tenants; when he steps on her prejudiced toes, though, she rejects him, complaining, "he's upset the balance around here" (231). The connecting of the immigrant with Christ is taken further when she spits out at the Priest, "as far as I'm concerned, Christ was just another D.P." (229)

In this way, O'Connor is able to juxtapose so-called Christianity with the real thing, Christ. Quick to expose the hypocrisy of the Bible Belt, she is just as eager to replace it with her view of the ideal religion. Flannery O'Connor "does believe that most Christians are kind of sentimental and do-gooders, and she's not interested in all that," Foote explains. She "says that religion does break and distort us and transcend us. And remakes us" (Barr 171). The Displaced Person, either the Pole or Christ, has been sent into the world to break, distort, transcend, and remake it—if the world will allow such conversion. Mrs. McIntyre refuses, and in the end she is locked in "her place," unseeing, unsaying, unredeemed.

As Foote adheres strictly to O'Connor's work in his adaptation, there seems little here for him to distort or remake, either. However, besides the Southern setting with its typically a-typical characters to whom he is sure to relate in O'Connor's collection, in two particular ways, he finds an affinity with O'Connor's world. The first, rather insignificant, but obvious in the Foote canon, is the appreciation of family graveyards. Mrs. McIntyre maintains the estate cemetery, and Foote shows her visiting the grave of her late husband. This is original to O'Connor's story, but it would be unlike Foote to neglect calling attention to it in his screenplay, as it is spotlighted so often in his own work.

The other area Foote calls attention to in the midst of the turmoil of the McIntyre world is the Priest's insistence on talking about the Heavenly Father and His Son: "For when God sent his Only Begotten Son, Jesus Christ Our Lord as a

Redeemer to mankind" (229), the Priest begins, only to be cut off by Mrs. McIntyre's impatient reference to Christ as another displaced person. Here the theme of fathers and sons that runs through most of Foote's work is elevated into the spiritual realm, as one sees Christ, the Son, separating himself from his heavenly Father in order to redeem the world. Similarly, the Displaced Person is separated from his family in Europe, coming to the Southern farm to redeem the "sinners" there. Both he and Christ are rejected and crucified in one fashion or another by those who refuse to let him/Him change their lives. Though Foote is careful to submerge "the sacred in the profane," this spiritual reference to fathers and sons is not out of place in his work and deserves mentioning here.

In spite of his past experience with adaptation, or maybe because of it, Foote has agreed to bring two other translations of other authors' works to the screen. In progress are an adaptation of Bette B. Lord's novel *Spring Moon* for Alan J. Pakula and Flaubert's *Madame Bovery*, a Roland Joffe production for HBO and BBC television (Wood xxvii-xxviii). While neither seems to have much in common with Foote's themes or styles, if past adaptations are any indication, one can speculate that these family-related themes will be spotlighted in one way or another.

Notes

Part I

1. Foote recalls his introduction to Faulkner's work stemmed from reviews he read of a French production of *As I Lay Dying*. After reading the novel, Foote recommended the work as a possible ballet to choreographer Valerie Bettis, for whose company the dance-play proved successful for many years.

2. Foote decided that "Old Man's" logistics were not his problem; he would "write it and it would be up to them to do it." The flood setting required enormous tanks of water in which stars Geraldine Page and Sterling Hayden nearly drowned in rehearsal. The heavy tanks seriously cracked the foundations of the CBS studio (Personal communication 11/14/87).

3. Faulkner uses the interior monologue extensively in such works as *The Sound and the Fury* (with Quentin Compson), *Absalom, Absalom* (with Miss Rosa), and *Light in August* (with Joe Christmas), just to mention a few.

4. The University Press of Mississippi published in 1985 a book which included Faulkner's short story, Foote's 1960 adaptation for television's Playhouse 90, and the 1972 film script adapted nearly verbatim from Foote's teleplay. Bruce Kawin, an authority on Faulkner films, included a discussion of Foote's work with the story in his *Faulkner and Film*, and Jack Barbera's "Tomorrow and Tomorrow and *Tomorrow*" is one of a few critical reviews of these three versions of the story. Finally, in "*Tomorrow*: The Genesis of a Screenplay," Foote himself has expounded on his experiences in adapting Faulkner's "Tomorrow." The stage adaptation in 1963 did not see production until 1968; because it follows the film version nearly verbatim, it will not be discussed separately in this study.

5. Kawin argues that Foote's *Tomorrow* focuses on the "romance" between Fentry and Sarah, only hurriedly summarizing Fentry's relationship with Jackson and Longstreet (65); I contend that Fentry's motivation for the "romance" is his desire to have a son and family as the end of the script bears out.

Part II

6. *To Kill a Mockingbird*, directed by Robert Mulligan for Universal in 1962, stars Gregory Peck as Atticus, a role which won him the Best Actor Academy Award that year. Mary Badham as Scout, Philip Alford as Jem, and John Megna as Dill are featured in the cast.

7. Dill's Aunt Stephanie joins the children in this scene, frightening her nephew, who is mesmerized by Jem's "horror" story about Boo Radley, nearly out of his wits. When she asks, "Dill, what are you doing here?" and he gasps out, "My Lord, Aunt Stephanie, you almost gave me a heart attack," Foote demonstrates the subtle humor that lies beneath the surface of many of his works. It is the most comic scene in the entire film and entirely Foote's creation.

Part III

8. *Hurry Sundown*, directed and produced by Otto Preminger for Paramount in 1966, starred Michael Caine as Henry Warren and Jane Fonda as Julie Warren. Other members of the cast include Faye Dunaway and Burgess Meredith.

9. *The Stalking Moon* starred Gregory Peck as Sam Varner and Eva Marie Saint as Sarah. It was distributed by Warner Brothers in 1968.

10. The musical adaptation of *Gone with the Wind* opened at the Drury Lane Theatre in London May 3, 1972.

11. *The Displaced Person* was directed by Glenn Jordan and produced by Matthew N. Herman. Irene Worth, as Mrs. McIntyre, and John Housman, as the Priest, starred. The cast also included Shirley Stoler, Lane Smith, and Robert Earl Jones.

Chapter Four

"A Voice of His Own": The Original Screenplays

Part I
The Traveling Lady **and** *Baby the Rain Must Fall*

After viewing Foote's adaptation of Faulkner's "Old Man," Roger Fristoe, film critic of the Louisville *Courier-Journal*, mused, "What a pity such a wonderful writer doesn't have a voice of his own" (SBTS), unaware of the myriad of plays Foote had written. His wish to hear the voice of this "wonderful writer" has been granted at least by the several original screenplays Foote has had filmed, not to mention *The Orphans' Home* cycle.

Gary Edgerton has written a succinct study of Foote's film career in an article for *Literature/Film Quarterly*, "A Visit to the Imaginary Landscape of Harrison, Texas: Sketching the Film Career of Horton Foote." The article highlights the contribution Foote has made to independent film making and the unique stamp his work has left on the history of American motion pictures. Citing Arthur Knight, author of *The Liveliest Art*, Edgerton calls attention to the recent American trend in on-location shooting which has resulted in an unheard of "three out of every four American movies" being made outside of Hollywood. Edgerton concludes that "the most important consequence of this development . . . is a corresponding upswing in independent film and video work across America" (2).

Stating that "indigenous filmmakers are now flourishing throughout America," Edgerton singles out Horton Foote as the "most intriguing and remarkable member of this renaissance," and, coupled with John Sayles, the "most prolific and accomplished practitioner." Labeling Foote as the "movement's elder statesman," Edgerton acknowledges Foote's age and "generational perspective" as part of what makes Foote's film work unique; Foote's contemporaries, he claims, "are either a vital part of the Hollywood establishment, or are no longer making motion pictures." He praises the "richness and integrity" which Foote infuses in his films, concluding that this "is a vivid indication of how much can be achieved when a talented film artist is attuned to his instincts and can focus his intentions and resolve" (3).

Outlining Foote's early theatre and film career, Edgerton divides Foote's motion picture work into two eras, citing the credits Foote received for film work between 1956 and 1968, most in the form of adaptation of his own or others' works. As the adaptations of others' work have been dealt with previously, this chapter will cover those films adapted from Foote's own original material, as well as the original screenplays. Examination of these screenplays continues the illumination of Foote's concentration on family, calling attention to his unique approach to character established earlier. It reveals, too, the realistic, yet positive perspective from which Foote's plays generally have been written.

Baby the Rain Must Fall, adapted from Foote's own stage play, *The Traveling Lady* (1954), was the first of the original adaptations, coming to the screen in 1964.[1] The primary focus of both the play and the screenplay, like most of Foote's work, is on the relationship between parents and their children, highlighting the misery created in broken families and by parents with demented ideas about child-rearing. The unbreakable cycle resulting from neglect and twisted methods of bringing up children is Foote's strongest message in the two works.

Baby the Rain Must Fall follows the search of a young woman named Georgette for her husband, Henry Thomas, who has just been released from prison after six years of incarceration. As her attempts to reunite her little girl, Margaret Rose, with the father who has never seen his child prove unsuccessful,

"A Voice of His Own": The Original Screenplays 91

Georgette travels on with a more family-oriented man by the name of Slim, enjoying both the traveling and the possibilities of a family in the new relationship.

Foote wrote the screenplay; therefore the plot follows the original stage play quite closely, although there are subtle changes in characterization between the two scripts. To avoid redundancy, this discussion will concentrate on the film version first, as it is the more widely known of the two, calling attention to similarities and differences between it and the play as they occur. Working with producer Alan J. Pakula and director Robert Mulligan, Foote recalls the filming as "a happy affair" (Edgerton 7); the three had worked together successfully on previous occasions.[2]

Shot in black and white, the film maintains a somewhat sinister atmosphere, particularly in those scenes focusing on the relationship between Henry Thomas and his foster mother Miss Kate Dawson, as the sadism of Miss Kate's methods of child-rearing comes to life in the foreboding shadows on the screen.[3] The negative results of such parental influence are far-reaching even into one's adulthood is the point Foote hones through his development of these characters in *Baby the Rain Must Fall*.

Although the film opens to reveal Georgette's journey to meet Henry, Foote shifts the emphasis from "the traveling lady" to her husband for the greater portion of the movie to illustrate the ill effects of Henry's upbringing. Miss Kate, who reared Henry from the age of ten when she took him in as an orphan, has taken the Biblical instruction of "Spare the rod, spoil the child" to the extreme and employed a punishing, Puritanical approach in his training. The local judge remembers, "Miss Kate . . . used to beat that Thomas boy . . . until the neighbors would complain. . . . She said she had to whip him to break his spirit" (12). The final words Miss Kate spits at Henry from her deathbed sum up her method of child-rearing, as well as her opinion of her foster child: "You're no good, Henry," she gasps, as he sits respectfully silent by her side. "You never have been. You're not worth killing."

The film reveals that this sadistic bent toward punishment, coupled with a personal disinterest in the boy's childhood, may have led to deep-seated psychological problems in Henry's adulthood. Afraid to reveal his resentment of her discipline, Henry has hidden his rage from his foster mother, but it erupts in other ways: not only can he not seem to avoid barroom brawls, Henry has just spent six years in prison for stabbing a man. Released from prison into the custody of his guardian, Henry fears Miss Kate's disapproval more than he fears returning to the penitentiary, as he cannot forget her cruelty to him as a child. He feels he must give up his dream of his own rock-a-billy band when she refuses to consent.

A relentlessly unloving parent-child relationship often breeds a violent response when the child becomes an adult, the film implies. Foote's point is brought to the forefront of the film particularly in the scenes following Miss Kate's death. Thinking he is now free from her dominance to pursue his musical career, Henry is furious to learn that Miss Kate's hold over him extends from the grave: she has left instructions with the sheriff to send Henry back to prison if he continues with his music. The montage of Henry tearing through her abandoned house and seeing the strap she used to whip him hanging inside the closet door climaxes in Henry's drunken visit to Miss Kate's freshly dug grave in the cemetery. A frenzied Henry desecrating the old woman's grave with a shovel and stabbing the dirt covering her body over and over with a knife is illustrative of the repressed pain and anger the young man has harbored against his guardian for nearly twenty years. Ironically, his outburst is enough to cancel his hard-won liberty and send him back to prison, Miss Kate's control over Henry just as viable as when she was alive.

As in previous plays, Foote also alludes to the negative effects the absence of a father can have on a child in his description of Henry Thomas. Besides the problems caused by Miss Kate's methods of child-rearing, the lack of any true father-figure in Henry's life has crippled his development, as well. While the judge could have filled that role himself, he chose to remove himself from the scene as much as possible, allowing Miss Kate free rein with Henry's upbringing. In the screenplay, the judge admits he gave the homeless Henry to Miss Kate in lieu of placing him in an orphanage, because "it seemed like the best thing to do at the time." The film even intimates that the judge was equally sadistic; Henry recalls the judge laughing at Henry's fear of Miss Kate. When Miss Kate dies, the judge, along with the sheriff, sees to it that her manipulation of Henry's life continues.

It is on the point of Henry's response to his upbringing that the play and film differ. Although the play shares the film's description of Henry's background, *The Traveling Lady* shows Henry appreciative of the discipline he received from Miss Kate's beatings. Sincerely sorrowful at her death, he confesses: "She was the only mother I ever knew . . . She could be hard . . . but I know now it was for my own good" (25). Another difference between the film and play surfaces when Henry points out that Miss Kate was pleased to see him return to his music: "She'd rather hear me sing than eat. . . . Miss Kate used to say, '. . . You've got a call to sing and that don't come to everybody'" (25).

This display of Miss Kate's interest in Henry is a marked difference between the two versions and reveals the change in perspective Foote's work has demonstrated from the early works, with their optimistic approach, to the later material, with its darker view of society. The later works also have a tendency toward open-endedness, as opposed to many of the earlier plays, which ended with every problem resolved. Further, in the later works, the cause of a character's suffering is not always explained. *Baby the Rain Must Fall* suggests that either Foote's insight into human nature has matured since he wrote *The Traveling Lady* or society, as Foote sees it, has changed from a caring community to a more selfishly motivated institution.

Henry's is not the only suffering revealed in *Baby the Rain Must Fall*. His wife Georgette, who has waited patiently for their reconciliation, raising their daughter alone, allows herself to open up to her husband again, only to have her love and trust snatched away as he is taken back to prison. That she, too, was the victim of a broken home is revealed when the play provides additional insight into Georgette's past, detailing her unfulfilled life with her father after her mother died. When asked why her own father has not helped her, Georgette explains, "My daddy? Oh, . . . I wouldn't ask him. I sent him a picture of Margaret Rose . . . an' he didn't even write to thank me" (18-19). Later she illustrates her father's insensitivity: "I always wanted a tree in our yard when I was a little girl. I used to beg Papa to plant one, but he couldn't listen. He'd had cotton growing up to the front door if he'd had his way" (42).

Foote realistically shows that an unhappy childhood sometimes results in a productive and happy adulthood, as some abused or neglected children are determined not to repeat the mistakes their parents made. While Henry's upbringing restricts him from developing beyond his experience, Georgette's gives her a commitment to do otherwise: she attempts to overcome her past by providing better care for her daughter. Though this effort would have better chances of success with a father-figure in the home, Georgette, like many of Foote's mother-characters, has to be both parents to the child. Unlike other Foote women who failed in the attempt, Georgette demonstrates that her best efforts have resulted in a loving relationship between her and Margaret Rose.

Foote intimates the necessity for children to have fathers of which they can be proud, and Georgette's awareness of this need is illustrated through her careful handling of the uneasy subject of Henry's past. It is important to Georgette that her little girl not know a father like her own, and she worries that Henry will turn out to be a disappointing father. Margaret Rose is full of questions about the mysterious missing person in her life, but her mother is careful not to expose Henry's shameful past to his daughter, telling her only that he is a singer away on a long trip.

Although in the play Henry never has the opportunity to settle in with the members of his family, and the indication is given that he has little intention of ever reuniting them, the movie develops a growing relationship between Henry and Georgette, and between Margaret Rose and her parents. Moreover, to demonstrate that Henry has potential to be what Georgette's father was not, the film shows Henry planting a tree with his little girl, a symbol of the growing new love the father and daughter share. Foote again presents an awareness that the influence of poor parenting is difficult to shed, however, when Henry takes that same shovel he used to plant a new life and uses it to dig up Miss Kate's grave in an attempt to destroy a past that refuses to die. All hope for a new life with his recovered family withers, as Henry is arrested and separated from his family once more.

In the scene in the film where Henry is removed from his wife and child, he is overcome with remorse and sadness, feelings generated by the time he has spent nurturing his newfound relationships. This scene loses most of its pathos in the play, as Henry has never laid eyes on his child until that moment when he bids her farewell; the parting is obviously superficial as no bond has been allowed to develop between the father and child. Further, the father-role is easily filled by another man, Slim, the deputy sheriff who has been as much a father to the child as Henry was. Slim plans to leave town with Georgette, hoping she will consent to marry him, and Georgette agrees to change her destination to accommodate his offer of a new chance at love and family life.

From *The Traveling Lady*, one gets the impression that Georgette is just "there for the ride," more interested in travel than in her family. "From Lovelady to Tyler, from Tyler to Harrison, from Harrison to the Valley," she muses at the end. "Margaret Rose, we sure do get around" (66). The tragedy of the broken family does not seem to make a deep impression on her. The play suggests that since Georgette has never been allowed to establish any kind of family life herself, the break-up of her marriage is an accepted—even expected—stage in her already disjointed life, thus supporting again Foote's commentary on the lasting effects of poor parent-child relationships. What is even sadder, and equally supported, is that Margaret Rose, through her father's insensitivity and weakness, is following in her mother's footsteps.

The film's ending cannot so neatly toss aside the growing, vibrant relationship it has shown developing in the Thomas family. For even though the film has allowed Slim an even more caring role with the Thomas family than in the play, it would be ludicrous, in such a short length of time, for him to propose to Georgette; nor would she be in any position to consider such an offer, as the film clearly has demonstrated a deep love between her and her husband. Also, while Margaret Rose probably would thrive under the loving kindness of a man such as Slim, she may not be able to erase so easily the memory of the man who sang for her and with whom she planted a chinaberry tree for a long, long while. The scene depicting Margaret Rose planting a tree by herself after her father's last arrest is significant and poignant, for all the promise of her enduring it also offers. It illustrates Foote's reluctance, however, to give up completely on optimistic possibilities. Foote leaves the ending of the film open, too, suggesting that reconciliation, at least for some, may be possible.

The final scene of the film, however, undermines the hope of reunion as it shows Slim's car, in which Georgette and Margaret Rose are riding, passing the patrol car which is taking Henry to prison, the opposite direction from his family's destination. This last impression also underscores the ambiguity of to whom the title song refers. For although Henry is the one who sings, "Baby, the rain must fall./ Baby, the wind must blow./ Wherever my heart leads me,/ Baby, I must go," it is obvious he is being taken against his will, as he has been his entire life. Georgette, equally a victim of uncaring parents, is going where she has to go, too, rather than where her heart is leading, forced there by her husband's inability to keep the family together.

What is clear in both *The Traveling Lady* and *Baby the Rain Must Fall* is Foote's depiction of unacceptable family relations and his implication that all the trouble in the story stems from absent or uncaring parents or guardians. Because Henry was not brought up in a nurturing atmosphere, there is little reason to believe that he will be able to provide that for his own family. "The child is father of the man," in that what one learns as a child shapes what one will be when as a parent. It is a continuous cycle, Foote suggests, and one in which the child's well-being is always at stake.

Part II
The Chase: Three Genres in One

Between the adaptations of *Hurry Sundown* (1966) and *The Stalking Moon* (1969), Foote found time to bring another of his own original works, *The Chase*, to the screen in 1966. *The Chase* is unique among Foote work in that it is his only story to exist in three genres: play, novel, and screenplay; additionally, it is Foote's sole contribution to the novel form.[4] This study will examine the three forms chronologically as written, for the evolution of *The Chase* from 1948 to 1966 illustrates the development of Foote's darker vision of society. The earlier version concludes more hopefully than the later ones. Begun as a stage play in 1948, *The Chase* introduces the story of Sheriff Hawes and his desire to maintain peace and compassion in the Texas community of Richmond, which is racked with hysteria over escaped convict Bubber Reeves. The relationship Hawes tries to establish with Bubber is reminiscent of other fathers and their prodigal sons in Foote's plays, especially as Foote demonstrates the universality of the situation.

Foote provides insight into each character in an attempt to explain motivations more fully and to elicit the sympathy of the audience for the characters in spite of, or because of, their situations. This is important particularly to Foote's depiction of the unsuccessful methods Bubber Reeves' mother has employed in her son's upbringing, as it demonstrates not only Foote's philosophy of child-rearing, but also his charity toward those who have been misguided in their approach. These are two characteristics of Foote's work that set it apart from the majority of American play writing.

Reminiscent of Henry Thomas in *Baby the Rain Must Fall*, Bubber Reeves is a willful child whose mother tried to break his rebellious spirit. Her efforts were met with his committing one crime after another, which drove her to wits' end and her son from one prison to another. She mourns to the Sheriff:

> I did the best I could. I tried whippin' him. I tried to shame him. I kept him home. I dressed him like a girl to keep him home. I never gave him money unless he worked for it. I prayed like the preachers

told me. I did whatever people said would help. I ask you to think back—what didn't I do? What else could I have done? (28)

Though many of her methods mirror Miss Kate's in *Baby the Rain Must Fall*, unlike Miss Kate, Mrs. Reeves seems truly to care for her son and acknowledges the ineffectuality of her misguided methods. She wavers between giving her son what he wants, aiding his escapes from the penitentiary and bribing the various officials, and trying to meet his deep-seated needs by giving him the honest and compassionate treatment he really yearns for by sending him back to the prison. This confused method of upbringing has had its effect in twisting her son's view of both the law and his relationship with his mother. One minute she tells him, "I hope he [Hawes] catches you. I'd rather see you hangin' in the courthouse square dead, than goin' on like this," and then "I didn't mean that, son! Forgive me for sayin' that. Honey, listen to your old mother. Give me the gun. Promise me you'll get out of here" (19).

Foote's belief that such confusion in child-rearing results in only frustrating a child all the more is borne out in Bubber's rebellious reactions to his mother's direction and his unfeeling response to her sporadic affection. He comes running home to her whenever he is in need of assistance, but only out of necessity. Receiving mixed signals about love and punishment all his life, Bubber assumes his mother never really loved him and resents her attempts at discipline.

Mrs. Reeves has made the same mistaken assumption about Hawes, associating him with all the previous sheriffs who insisted that she beat the meanness out of her son, rather than try to love him into change and repentance. She accuses Hawes of wanting to kill her son, and when her attempt to bribe him fails, she screams, "I hate you! I hope they have to chase the child your wife is carryin'. . . I hope your child is hunted and killed some day" (29).

Representing Foote's exemplary father-figure, both in the home and the neighborhood, Hawes understands the love a parent has for a child, no matter what that child may have done, and has no intention of killing Bubber. Instead, he comes to connect the boy he is chasing with his own unborn child, as Mrs. Reeves already has suggested, and his blending the two children together in his mind reflects Foote's universal philosophy on family and how the private sector can influence the larger community. Longing to quit his job as sheriff to concentrate on raising his own family, Hawes sighs, "I want to live in peace now with my wife and baby an' let other people live in peace" (12-13), favorably suggesting the kind of father he will be when given the chance.

When Mrs. Reeves realizes that Hawes is acting in the best interest of her son, she demonstrates her love for her son by begging the sheriff to save Bubber from the lynch mob; when Hawes has Bubber surrounded, though, she interferes again. Running at Bubber as he emerges from the hide-out cabin, she confuses the sheriff, causing him accidentally to kill the unarmed convict. The full impact of her failure to rear her son effectively is illustrated in Bubber's death and Mrs. Reeves' grief. "How'm I gonna find peace? How'm I gonna rest?" (57), she mourns. Having ruined her chances with her son, she faces a torturous life of regrets. Foote's commentary on such confused parent-child relationships is bleak but firm; that she had to handle her son without a father-figure in the home may explain part of her inadequacy, but it does not excuse it in Foote's estimation. Still, Foote is careful to elicit sympathy for Mrs. Reeves in her reaction to her son's death, taking the sting out of his criticism of her parenting methods.

Foote's point that the community suffers when the family fails is unavoidable, especially in the sheriff's reaction to the role he has been forced to play in the local tragedy. Even more distraught than the mother, Hawes chastens himself with, "The chase is over and I've lost" (59). But Foote, ever eager to suggest the positive in the early plays, is quick to offer hope for the future in the conclusion of the 1948 version of *The Chase*. Accentuating this optimism, Hawes' wife reminds him that the chase did not start or end just that night, and she urges him to "Keep on livin'. Keep on tryin'" (59). The late introduction of another uncontrollable child in the community whom the sheriff agrees to counsel reinforces the cyclical, continuous pattern of life: the chase is not over, and though Hawes may have lost this one particular battle, he has not lost the entire war. It is Foote's intention that the audience realize that with father-figures like Sheriff Hawes in the community, there is the promise of victory.

When Foote found time on his hands in the mid-1950's, he expanded the play into a novel of some 274 pages, fleshing out characters and exposing motivations more deeply.[5] The novel follows the basic plot set out in the play, but a few characters are added, each one highlighting the parent-child theme of the earlier work more brightly, while putting the relationship of Bubber and his parents (Mr. Reeves is added in the novel) in sharper relief. The first of these additional characters opens the novel: Miss Mattie, a spinster, whose life has been dominated by her mother to the point of near desperation. Foote's plays, as discussed previously, often offer an examination of the ill effects of manipulative parents; Mattie and her mother are a case in point. Foote tells us that Mattie is not afraid of her domineering mother, but that "it made life so much easier if she didn't cross her" (3). For that reason, Mattie has allowed her mother to choke out any social life she might have enjoyed; this acquiescence to her mother's will has chained Mattie figuratively (though almost literally) to her mother's side in the hotel room that has been their home since Mattie was ten. At one point in the novel, Mattie's true feelings are exposed:

> She thought of her Papa, lying in the graveyard. She thought of death and what it would be like when she died or her mother died and she was finally alone . . . And she felt the old bitterness rise again in her heart against her mother. She'd always blamed her mother for her failure to marry . . . and she thought: Die, Mama and leave me free (136-137).

The loss Mattie feels for her father echoes through her thoughts, and speculations of what might have been had he lived are subtle but present in her reveries. That her mother had to add his responsibilities to her own is another point Foote has included in works incessantly, providing insight into the mother's mistakes and explaining, though not excusing, the mother's motivations. The image of a hotel as poor substitute for a home is also one of Foote's common motifs, symbolizing the disintegration of the family when the parents can no longer maintain their proper roles.

Foote calls to attention the necessity for proper priorities in parent-child relations, as the reality that her mother is all she has now frightens the aging spinster. "Hard as it was," Foote writes, "it was better than being completely alone, . . . and she quickly whispered, 'Don't die, Mama. . . . I didn't mean that'" (137). Regardless who is to blame for this unhealthy relationship, it is too late to rectify the situation, and Mattie clings with childish terror to a mother she should have long outgrown.

Mattie and her mother serve as an interesting contrast to Bubber and his mother, another domineering parent who tried to shape her child's life to her own will. In Bubber's case, however, his will is not so pliable as Mattie's. His reaction is illustrative of the opposite extreme: he turned to crime and violence whenever he could. Foote suggests once again that the presence of a father-figure in a family can provide balance in a child's upbringing; in the novel Mrs. Reeves, whose husband has been there to support her, does not appear so confused or drastic in her methods of child-rearing as her prototype in the play. However, Mr. Reeves has left most of the upbringing to his wife, and his drinking problem and lack of involvement in his son's life may be the underlying reason behind Bubber's rebellion. Indifferent fathers can be just as damaging as no father at all, Foote intimates here, as in previous works.

The novel follows the play closely, with Mrs. Reeves soliciting the sheriff's help on his own terms, just so Bubber is taken alive. Like most mothers, she believes her boy is good at heart and holds out for the slim chance that, if given the opportunity, he might repent. "'I'll change him and save him,'" she promises, "'because I love him. . . . In spite of everything he has done'" (115). Because he has been shown more affection than his counterpart in the play, the Bubber of the novel seems to have more feeling for his mother. When his mother informs Bubber that for the first time, for his own good, she cannot help him escape, however, he proves one evening of good intentions cannot erase years of misguided discipline.

"'All right. Go. I'll hate you. I'll curse you until the day I die'" (157), he rejects her, as he escapes into the night.

After Bubber is killed and they have him buried by his baby sister, Mrs. Reeves blames herself for trying too hard to mold her son after her image. "'I always wanted a boy the town could be proud of,'" she admits to her husband. "'I killed him trying to make him be someone they could be proud of'" (238-239). Whether or not Foote agrees with Mrs. Reeves summation of Bubber's situation is unclear; his approval of the gentler approach to child-rearing, though, is presented here. If Henry Thomas in *Baby the Rain Must Fall* was not illustration enough, surely Bubber Reeves is. But to soften the rather harsh portrait of the Reeves painted in both play and novel, Foote adds a scene at the family graveyard, his typical symbol of reconciliation and forgiveness. The Reeves choose to remain in their old community to be close to their dead children and to tend their graves; this gesture earns them forgiveness in Foote's work.

Sheriff Hawes' character in the novel is similar to that of the play, and his role as father-figure to Bubber is just as prominent, continuing Foote's depiction of the ideal father. In the novel, however, Hawes already has a young son, S. P., and he is better able to understand Mrs. Reeves' feeling for Bubber, especially after he has accidentally killed her son: "And he thought again of his own son asleep in his bed. . . . and he thought of the love he had for the boy and the love Mrs. Reeves was bound to feel for her son and he began to cry again" (232-233). Only the thought of his family gives Hawes incentive to recover and the courage to forfeit the sheriff's job for the desired family farm. Here, finally, the former sheriff is able to give his son the attention he has longed to give:

> He knew that S. P. and Ruby were happier, much happier than they were at the jail and that meant a great deal to him. He and S. P. for the first time in their lives were able to spend time together. Whenever the boy was home from school, he would follow after his father around the farm, working along with him and they would share in minutest detail what they had done while apart that day (265).

Though he may have failed in his attempt to "save" Bubber, Hawes proves he will be the kind of father his son needs by spending time with the boy and allowing a bond to develop between them. This is the father-son relationship of which Foote approves.

The generational tie from father to son is an important connection to Foote's concept of the well-rooted family, as it can provide the solidarity necessary for successful future families. To illustrate, Foote adds Hawes' thoughts on his own dead father in the novel. The sheriff longs to buy back his father's farm, dreaming that regaining his father's land will resurrect his father and their time together. Foote writes, "He wanted to be a boy again, following his father behind the long rows of cotton, . . . petted and taken care of and be loved and protected" (109). It is natural for the adult to look back with longing for the security of a well-nourished father-child union, and Foote holds up Hawes and his thoughts of his father in contrast to the wayward, "fatherless" Bubber. But as an adult must shoulder familial responsibilities, Hawes closes his mind to his desires, recalling his duty to his own son and wife for which his father prepared him. He is careful to honor his father by decorating his grave, though, in true Foote fashion.

Unlike the play, when another mother complains of trouble with her son and solicits the aid of the authorities, in the novel Hawes has already resigned his position, and, rather than try to make restitution for the failure with Bubber by taking on another juvenile delinquent's case, Hawes leaves the problem to the new sheriff. Any penance Hawes will do will be with his own son. This minor departure from the original story is significant, in that it suggests a narrower vision on Foote's part: the novel suggests that all any one father can hope to accomplish is with his own individual family; the community's family is too much to ask of any one man. This apparent change in philosophy will not prove to be permanent in Foote's canon, but it is interesting to note the differences between the 1948 and the 1956 versions of *The Chase*.

In 1965, producer Sam Spiegel purchased Foote's novel *The Chase* for filming, under the direction of Arthur Penn. Although Foote had worked with Penn when he was writing for television, he was unable to agree with Penn's interpretation of the work and withdrew from the script writing early in the production. Lillian Hellman was secured to finish the screenplay, and she receives total screen credit for writing, even though Foote did return to edit the script before the project was complete. It is difficult to determine whose work is which, as the film follows the novel faithfully up to the final episodes.[6] Foote, however, was very displeased with the final outcome; he comments, "Lillian Hellman did the screenplay. She said that she used my novel and my play as a departure, and then she departed. . . . I wasn't too happy with her" (Edgerton 7). Later, Foote mused ruefully, "I felt like the mother of Moses — I couldn't do anything; I'd given my baby away!" (Personal communication 11/14/87)

Actually, in spite of the melodramatic flavor of many scenes, the film version of *The Chase* does not depart too much from Foote's original story until the final scenes of the movie. The parent-child relationships Foote established in the earlier *Chase* manuscripts between both Bubber and Hawes (called Calder in the film) and Bubber and his parents remains intact, and nearly every character at one point or another in the film discusses the importance of "family." Still, the emphasis placed by Foote on this theme in all his work, and particularly in both play and novel versions of *The Chase*, is reduced by the different approach taken by both producer Spiegel and director Penn, as well as co-author Lillian Hellman.

The relationship between Bubber and his mother does not suffer much redirection in the film. As in both play and novel, in the film Mrs. Reeves confesses, "I've done so many wrong things to him [Bubber], I want to help him," and she convinces her husband to help her with Bubber, because "no matter what happens, he's our son." But Bubber, who appears in the movie as an abused victim, always "in the wrong place at the wrong time," is indifferent to her last-minute compassion; he turns for understanding instead to his wife Anna, who, unlike in the play or novel, still loves Bubber and wants to help him, even though she has been having an affair with Jake Rogers since Bubber's departure. Jake and his wealthy father Val Rogers are two new characters to Foote's story. In spite of his money, all Val really cares about is his only son's happiness.

He mourns that his son is "always running away from me," and his plans to build a local college are so that other parents' sons will not have to go away to school as his boy did. "I love Jake," Val admits to Sheriff Calder. "Maybe I love him too much." Val's deep commitment to his son would be admirable in Foote's eyes, yet the inevitable tendency to meddle in one's children's lives is a parental flaw which the author has criticized in past works.

While Jake admires his father and wants to please him, he does not appreciate his father's interference in keeping him from marrying the only girl he ever loved—Anna, Bubber's wife. When Jake dies in the riot the town creates in their attempt to lynch Bubber, Val's life is essentially over, too. He has to live with the memory of his son's last words, telling him how much he had loved Anna and wanted to marry her. Once again, in Foote-fashion, children's lives are ruined by parents' manipulation; in this case, though, the father will pay for his interference the rest of his grieving life.

What can be said for Jake and his father, of course, can be said also for Bubber and his mother. Mrs. Reeves draws the connection herself when she screams, "I love my son as much as he [Val Rogers] loves his son." Both family's relationships are held up for scrutiny, and neither passes Foote's test. The necessity for moderation in child-rearing, neither too much indulgence nor too much punishment, is again Foote's point.

The film gives in to the Hollywood penchant for sexual innuendo that Foote sidesteps in his writing; and an emphasis on "chasing" throughout the film also seems to detract from Foote's purpose, as his intention was to write an "anti-chase" script in protest against Hollywood's infatuation with action films (Personal communication 11/14/87). These departures from Foote's direction seem minor, however, when compared to the melodramatic, violent, and action-packed changes made in the story's ending. After Bubber is cornered in a secluded junkyard (a modern equivalent to Foote's cemeteries?), he is gunned down on the courthouse steps by a member of the mob, in spite of the sheriff's attempts to protect him. As in the original story, the sheriff fails, but here it is not because of a weakness on his part but because he is one against many who do not share his pacifist perspective.

The film version of *The Chase* clearly presents a darker portrayal of society and human nature in keeping with Foote's later work, but whether or not this is Foote's intention is unclear. Terry Barr suggests, however, that producer Sam Spiegal was responsible for the film's frenzied climax. He quotes film historian Bernard F. Dick's commentary on Spiegal's purpose in changing Foote's ending:

> [Sam Spiegel] envisioned a film with assassination as a controlling but sunken metaphor; he wanted the climax to evoke President Kennedy's assassination without making reference to it. . . . He also believed that, in the mid-1960's, audiences would accept a film portraying an America whose amber waves of grain had been singed by the fires of violence. President Johnson had escalated the Vietnam War. . . . It was the right time to take Horton Foote's parable . . . and turn it into an allegory of an America that kills what it does not understand (Barr 200).

Most critics seemed aware and appreciative of Spiegal's intentions, and, perhaps for that reason, the film has remained popular since its premiere. Foote, however, does not appreciate the added political interpretation to his work (Barr 200) and is quick to dismiss the film as "another Hollywood lesson to realize—what can happen to material that's turned over to somebody else" (Edgerton 7). He would be careful to keep from making that mistake again, as in the future he would maintain control over the filming of his work. "I have only seen it [the film version of *The Chase*] once," Foote insists, "and I have no idea about it. It has nothing to do with my play" (Wood, LFQ 228).

Part III
The *Tender Mercies* of Independent Film Making

Following what he considers a fiasco (*The Chase*), Foote might have become completely soured on working in film had he not had the opportunity to bring his adaptation of Faulkner's *Tomorrow* to the screen in 1972. The work on *Tomorrow*, after years of what Foote would call hackwork for Hollywood, rekindled the film making relationship to which Fred Coe had introduced him in the early years. Foote recalls:

> I learned a great deal with *Tomorrow* (1972). . . . I learned that film really should be like theatre in the sense that in theatre, the writer is, of course, very dominant . . . If we don't like something, we can speak up our minds. . . . It is always a collaborative effort. . . . But in Hollywood it wasn't so. A writer there has in his contract that you are a writer for hire, which means that you write a script, then it belongs to them. Then they can do what they want to, shoot it the way they want. God forbid that you should ever try to get on the set. They don't want you. But here I was and I felt a part of it, and I felt very creative about film again (Edgerton 7-8).

This revitalized creativity for film resulted in *Tender Mercies* in 1983, Foote's first full-length original screenplay, for which he won a second Academy Award for screen writing and another Writers Guild Award.[7] The film "catapulted Horton Foote into the most active professional period in his life," Edgerton writes, "at the unlikely age of 67" (9). And since then, he continues, Foote has become "a forerunner and innovator in the resurgence of American independent film making during the present era" (5).

Pointing out that *Tender Mercies* cost "only 4.5 million dollars to make in an age when most Hollywood films cost three times as much," Barr sees the film as "Foote's determination to battle a Hollywood system that generally refuses to make such personal films" (213). The success of the film, and the bad experience with the adaptation of *The Chase* in 1966, led to Foote's decision to exercise full control over his productions. "I just feel you have to be in charge," he insists (Wood, *LFQ* 230). Now, if he cannot have total control over the script with final veto power, he refuses to do the film, Foote explains (Personal communication 11/14/87). It is not that he enjoys adversarial situations with actors, directors, or producers, but that his quarrel arises from their attempt "to reinterpret the play from their point of view. . . . As long as I'm living," Foote vows, "they'll never do it to my plays" (Personal communication 11/13/87).

Contrary to the popular rumor that Robert Duvall requested Foote write him a script, Foote recalls the original idea for the film was his own; he was in need of money for the independent production of his *Orphans' Home* cycle (Personal communication 11/14/87). Having watched his nephew struggle to succeed in the country-music business, Foote was initially interested in young boys starting a band of their own. He also draws a connection between these fledglings and himself as a young actor trying to find work (Barr 205). However, as the character of Mac Sledge, the older man who aids the boys in their climb, developed, Foote found himself increasingly more interested in him. Sledge was taken from Foote's recollection of an experienced musician who "had been through it all" and had offered his help to Foote's nephew. This gave Foote the background he needed for the story.

A deeply-etched impression from his own days on the stage when he observed how alcoholism can ruin a talented artist also figured into Foote's purpose as he wrote. "That's what I had in mind," Foote claims, recalling that "some have the humility and grace to fight it off and come back" (Sterritt 37). This desire to "come back" is prevalent in the screenplay; an in-depth study of the film indicates, too, that the age-old father-son theme, on both the earthly and spiritual levels, has never been more obvious in Foote's work. It is suggested, too, that in many ways, *Tender Mercies* exhibits an autobiographical connection with Foote, as the author enjoyed a renaissance with the production of *Tender Mercies* not unlike his protagonist's comeback as a musician and a human being.

Tender Mercies also demonstrates Foote's careful craftsmanship of character and his inclination to present each role realistically, yet charitably; no character comes across unsympathetically, regardless of his or her situation in the story. Finally, in many ways *Tender Mercies* is a new, more hopeful rewriting of *The Traveling Lady* and *Baby the Rain Must Fall*, as discussion of this film's details will show (see Wood, LFQ 235) where the central character, also a musician, gets a second chance to redeem his life.

Mac Sledge is a once-famous country musician whose life has been ruined by alcoholism. Taken in by the widow Rosa Lee, who manages the Maripasa Hotel in Texas where he has been staying, he is allowed to live there and work off his debt.

With her gentle ways and quiet belief in the "tender mercies" of God, Rosa Lee encourages Mac into giving up drinking, becoming a Christian, and eventually reviving his music career. Mac and Rosa Lee even marry, revitalizing the family unit she and her son "Sonny," as well as Mac, need.

The emphasis on the Christian family is stronger in this script than in any other Foote piece to this point, supporting the father-son theme and allowing the subtle spiritual underthought to surface more clearly than ever before. While the reestablishing of stability via family is noticeably important, it is also apparent that the replanting of roots is not enough to satisfy Mac's thirst to "be all that he can be." When his initial attempt to get back into the song writing business is momentarily thwarted by his ex-wife Dixie, Mac curses, "I don't give a Goddamn about any of this no more so what in hell is wrong with me?" His attempt to run away and return to drinking proves unsatisfactory, though, as he becomes aware that this is not what he is thirsting for; he pours out the whiskey he has bought and comes back to Rosa Lee who has been praying "Show me thy way, O Lord, and teach me thy paths."

A surprise visit from Sue Ann, his daughter from the former marriage to Dixie, brings the nature of Mac's thirsting into sharper focus, as the necessity for spiritual reconciliation with God and the need to rebuild one's family are combined. Everything Foote has suggested before in previous works about the importance of strong father-child relationships resurfaces here in *Tender Mercies* as Sue Ann, hearing of Mac's rehabilitation, tries wistfully to reunite with the man whose music has given her everything money can buy, except a family in which he could be her father.

Restricted from her father by her mother all her life, Sue Ann has had to create a father for herself from the negative scraps her mother has thrown her and a few, vague recollections she has of their early contact. She asks Mac to recall a song he used to sing her, but Mac pretends he has forgotten. When she leaves, however, Mac sings "On the Wings of a Snow White Dove" without faltering, fully understanding for the first time the combination of the familial and spiritual which has been lacking in his life for so long.

The lyrics of this song, as well as all the songs used in the film, are significant in interpreting the meaning of the film, for as Foote himself has pointed out, "the role of lyrics in *Tender Mercies*, and all the films, is very important" (Personal communication 11/13/87). Working with Robert Duvall, who wrote and sang many of the songs for the film, Foote chose each song carefully to underscore his theme. This particular song tells of God the Father blessing Jesus the Son at his baptism; as Mac sings softly to himself, "On the wings of a snow white dove/He sends his pure sweet love/A sign from above/On the wings of a dove," the love sign comes into clearer focus for Mac the father and Mac the son. Having already attended the Baptist church where Rosa Lee sings in the choir and where he himself has sung "Jesus Saves" without the aid of the hymnal, Mac is baptized (like Jesus in the song) along with his new step-son Sonny. As the preacher intones, "In the name of the *Father*, and the *Son*, and the Holy Spirit" (my emphasis), the spiritual interpretation of the relationship between fathers and sons emerges.

This reconciliation with God, of the earthly son with the heavenly Father, now clears the path for Mac to claim what even the successful man he was before could not have achieved: an inner peace that is not based on temporal things. When Sonny comments that neither of them looks different after their baptism, Mac's reply, "Not *yet*," intimates his belief that his reunion with God will lead to meaningful changes in his life. Now that his spiritual relationship with God is in order, he can see the way clear to reestablish his relationships with the people in his life, as well as develop his own potential for success as a man.

This perspective that Mac now holds on life is seen particularly in the way in which Mac views his alcoholic and sinful past, even though it may have proved financially successful for him at times. Foote has claimed that the whole film pivots on one statement Mac makes about who he is, and he recalls actually hearing a washed-up star speak those words which figure so importantly in *Tender Mercies* and sharpen the focus on the significance of the spiritual in this work (Personal communication 11/14/87; see also Barr 207). When, before his baptism and spiritual reconciliation, an old fan asked, "Were you really Mac Sledge?" Mac responded, "Yes, ma'am, I guess I *was*." The film suggests that through the washing away of the "old self" symbolically in baptism and literally in his changed lifestyle, now Mac can take sure-footed steps to *be* in fact the man Mac Sledge believes God intended him to be: a man who can restructure his role as husband and father now that his own role as "child" of God has been redefined, a man whose completeness no longer depends on the financial success and notoriety of what he has come to call "a dirty business."

Previous Foote work has emphasized that when one's private life is in order, the responsibility one owes the larger community can and should be met. As the younger men solicit Mac's help in establishing a local country band, their "you've been a real inspiration to us, Sir" confirms the father-figure role Mac has played unconsciously in their lives. Before his rehabilitation, Mac could only offer vague advice to the young men; now that he has straightened out his own priorities, though, he has more than mere words of "fatherly counsel" to give them. Teaming up with the five part-time musicians Mac aids the furthering of their careers with his talent for writing and singing. Following his own advice to them to "sing it the way you feel it," Mac's songs now reflect what Foote sees as the true nature of success, as Mac goes from writing such sad songs as "God Can Forgive Me, Why Can't You?" to more hopeful ones, such as "If You'll Just Hold the Ladder, Baby, I'll Climb to the Top."

While *Tender Mercies* has not avoided making a strong spiritual statement, it is Foote's inclination to temper any religious tenets with practical, human application. "Faith without works is dead," his scripts echo, and spiritual roots without growth in human relationships is useless to Foote's characters. Acknowledging Rosa Lee's role in his reversal from alcoholic to born-again Christian, the latter song illustrates: "Things just started changing with your touch./Yesterday, tomorrow, just isn't near as much./Now I'll be everything this man can be before I stop./If you'll just hold the ladder, baby, I'll climb to the top." Here, the need for love combined in both the familial and the spiritual in order for the refinement of the total man to be accomplished is clarified. It suggests, too, that the ladder held by his faithful wife not only leads to eternal fulfillment, but to earthly satisfaction, as well.

It is important in Foote's work that life be represented realistically. When his newly recovered relationship with Sue Ann is cut short by an automobile accident that takes her life, Mac quickly realizes that his life as a Christian is no more sheltered from this world's tragedies than it was before. Foote intimates that all relationships cannot be mended, some by choice and some by chance, and the poignancy of missed opportunities between fathers and their children on this earth is underlined in this scene. When all the hopes of making up for his lost time as a father to Sue Ann are erased, Mac's vision becomes momentarily clouded by the shock, and, like many of Foote's characters, Mac prays to know why such unexplained cruelties occur. In his grief, Mac even questions the purpose behind Rosa Lee's taking pity on him in the first place, concluding he does not "trust happiness—never did, never will." A recent interview revealed that this statement is one of Foote's own fears, as well; he himself puts his trust in more substantial things, Foote claims, suggesting a connection between the author and his character and offering insight into Foote's own intended interpretation of Mac Sledge (Wood, LFQ 232).

The necessity of learning from these life-altering experiences and using them for growth toward maturity is a conclusion at which Foote's plays have arrived before. Foote's quiet belief in the hope of reconciliation and healing, however, exudes more profusely at the conclusion of *Tender Mercies* than in any other work thus far. Though still immature in his understanding, Mac exhibits signs of growth even in his questioning, and Rosa Lee's quiet strength and maturity promise the support he may need along the way. He has come to appreciate the commitment she has made to him when she tells him, "I love you, you know, and every night when I say my prayers and I thank the Lord for his blessings and his tender mercies to me, you and Sonny head the list." He also recognizes the source of her strength and realizes that it is available for him, as well.

The end of the film bears this growth out, as Mac picks up the pieces and continues down the new road he has cut for himself with his second family and his second chance at life, rather than returning to his previous bitter and empty life. For while he may never have the chance to rectify all the mistakes of the past, the contentment he has found and the commitment he has made with his new family are more deeply rooted than he realizes, the film intimates, and will survive the storm of his present bereavement. The ending illustrates this as Mac, still singing "On the Wings of a Snow White Dove," continues to strengthen his bond with his new step-son by tossing a football with him. Although he may have allowed his initial role as father to go astray, there is hope for restitution in this second chance with Sonny. And as music in Foote's films reinforces his theme, the words of the final song, "You're the good things I threw away/coming back to me every day," promise the audience hopeful possibilities for this reformed man's life.

This optimistic conclusion is heightened when set in relief against the character of Dixie, Mac's unfulfilled (though financially successful) ex-wife. Dixie's success as a country singer has come from the songs Mac wrote for her years ago; unlike Mac, she has made no attempt to move forward in her life. Having cushioned her world and that of her daughter's with "everything money could buy," she has not accumulated happiness, nor has she sheltered her child from the realities of the world. In the face of calamity when her child is taken from her, she can only curse God for "doing this to me," as she fights and cries like the petulant child she is. Indeed, in the words of Mac's song she continues to wail, she is "still going crazy."

Though Foote is not unkind in his characterization of Dixie, sympathizing with her struggle to survive in spite of a ruined marriage, he does not turn the camera away from the reality of how many people mishandle life's situations in his depiction of this single parent. To further this point, the film offers the character of Rosa Lee to make a quiet but significant statement when compared to Dixie. Though not a successful singer or a glamorous wife, she provides the necessary stability and maturity to inspire Mac's conversion and growth. Though she takes no credit for her role in Mac's rebirth, her understated strength even impresses the jaded Sue Ann who had initially looked down on her for not being rich or fashionable. Rosa Lee's ability to go on, even after her first husband was killed in Viet Nam, and make a life for herself and her son, because of her trust in the "tender mercies" of God exposes the hollowness in Dixie's life, and her singing "Jesus, Savior Pilot Me" in the church choir serves as a symbolic contrast with Dixie's singing "The Best Bedroom in Town" in her stage show.

But Mac Sledge and his reconciliation as son and father is not the only life Foote focuses on in *Tender Mercies*, though it best illustrates the spiritual side of Foote's theme. A look at the half-orphaned Sonny and the renewal of a father-son team accentuates Foote's interest in the earthly side of his recurring theme. Having never known the father he lost in Viet Nam, Sonny attempts to conjure up an image of his father through old pictures and his mother's memories of things he was too young to retain. He wants desperately to create his own identity out of that of his father, keeping the picture of the man he never knew on his bedside table and proudly announcing to any who care to listen that he was named for his father, Carl Herbert Wadsworth. Even his nickname, "Sonny," suggests the intended relationship with his absent father.

When the boys at school taunt Sonny with "your Dad's dead," he comes home full of questions. He is disgusted that his mother does not know much about how his father died, though she does the best she can with the sketchy information she herself was given. Unlike Dixie, Rosa Lee recalls the good things about her first husband, informing her son that his father "was just a boy, but he was a good boy." Finally, Rosa Lee takes Sonny out to the cemetery where her first husband is buried, and though he was too young to attend the funeral, Sonny is impressed that a crowd of people came to pay their respects to his father. It is important that he know his father was someone others liked and admired. This visit to the grave is Foote's typical way of cementing a bond between family members.

Before allowing himself to trust Mac, it is important to Sonny that he appreciate Sonny's real father. When Sonny first makes Mac's acquaintance, he wants to know if the man ever knew his "daddy." When Mac replies he did not, Sonny persists, "Would you have liked him if you did?" Perhaps it is Mac's easy "Sure" that leads Sonny to place his trust and eventual love in the man who goes from being an alcoholic instructing him not to "throw stones at me, Son," in true prodigal style, to a reformed step-father Sonny can proudly claim.

When asked at Mac's comeback "concert" by a young friend if he likes Mac better than his own daddy, Sonny thoughtfully responds in the affirmative, explaining to his friend, "I never knew my own daddy," which in turn emphasizes the distinction between companionship and blood relationship Foote has pointed out before. Foote adds a bit of wry humor here, too, when the young friend, watching his own drunken father, confides to Sonny, "I know mine; he's not so much either."

Tender Mercies, Foote's own "comeback film," fulfills Foote's theme of father-child relationships on both the earthly and the spiritual plane and does so more explicitly than any other work to this point in Foote's career. It continues to demonstrate Foote's commitment to realism, as well, while at the same time reemphasizes Foote's unwavering belief in the promise of hope and reconciliation in spite of an acknowledgement of a more sordid society. And with the possible exception of *To Kill a Mockingbird*, this piece has received more praise than any other in Foote's canon. Interestingly enough, Universal, who released both *Tender Mercies* and *To Kill a Mockingbird*, disliked both films and did their utmost to keep them from being distributed in America. Foote dismisses this Hollywood attitude with, "Today the market is aimed at children of five—they should be writing the screenplays" (Personal communication 11/14/87). And though some critics also found the film ponderous and wearisome—one Paramount representative claimed it was "like watching paint dry" (Personal communication 11/14/87)—most critics and audience alike appreciated its simplicity and subtlety (CBY 146).

In "Let's Hear it for the Human Being," David Sterritt writes, "The excitement of *Tender Mercies* lies below the surface. It's not the quick change of fast action, the flashy performances or the eye-zapping cuts," he says. "Rather, it's something much more rare—the thrill of watching characters grow, personalities deepen, relationships ripen and mature" (36). Demonstrating how Foote's work takes Hollywood back to "decent films," Sterritt goes on to say, "It's the pleasure of rediscovering the dramatic richness of decency, honesty, and a few other qualities that have become rare visitors to the silver screen. It feels good to have them back again," he concludes.

Despite some seeing the journey as sentimental, the typical reaction of the modern cynic, Sterritt defends Foote's style, calling *Tender Mercies* "a daring picture" that has tossed "decades of Hollywood convention cheerfully out the window," while "deftly sidestep[ping] sentimentality" (36). Seeing *Tender Mercies* as the successful sign post of the current independent film making movement, Foote's friend and sometime producer Alan Pakula credits Foote for initiating this trend in thwarting the Hollywood tradition and making it feasible, when he reflects:

> He has a specific voice, a specific style, and he has never abandoned it, even though it has cost him. He has never cut his talent to the fashion of the time. And because he wrote his works, whether they were going to be produced or not, he got what most American writers don't get—a second act. You are seeing continuity and fruition now, because he has never wavered from his vision (Freedman 50).

Tender Mercies is clearly indicative of the vision Foote has never abandoned, as we see his theme of the prodigal son and the reconciliation with the father, ever present in all the preceding works, more clearly than ever before.

Part IV
The Successful *Trip[s] to Bountiful*

Following upon the heels of *Tender Mercies*' success, *The Trip to Bountiful*, originally a 1953 teleplay, was brought to the screen in 1985.[8] This play allows the father-child theme, as present here as in the other works, to take a less visible position than in *Tender Mercies* and brings the broader topic of "coming home" into the spotlight. Still, this homecoming relies on reconciliation on both the earthly and spiritual levels, the major theme that threads through all of Foote's work, weaving them together into one large tapestry. Regan Courtney, husband of Cynthia Clawson who sang "Softly and Tenderly" for the film, concurs that Foote wrote *The Trip to Bountiful* "to share a common longing for reconciliation and home" (SBTS), and many people agree that this work is Foote's most beautiful creation and the focal point of his mature vision. Serving as co-producer, Foote maintained complete control over the production, a precedent he had established with *Tender Mercies*. As the screenplay Foote wrote for the film follows the original stage script nearly verbatim, this study will discuss both scripts simultaneously.

The film begins with the strains of "Softly and Tenderly, Jesus is Calling," setting the stage for the theme of coming home to family, land, and God. Interestingly enough, the hymn was changed from "There's Not a Friend Like the Lowly Jesus" used in the stage script; this change emphasizes, perhaps, a calculation on Foote's part to draw immediate attention to the theme, since the earlier hymn does not suggest homecoming as the second one does. The background scene of a young mother chasing her small son through fields of bluebonnets, hugging him closely when she catches him, further illustrates the focus on familial reconciliation, as well.

Mrs. Carrie Watts is an old woman forced to live in a cramped apartment in Houston with her son Ludie and his wife, Jessie Mae. All she wants is to go home to the family "land of plenty," named "Bountiful" by her grandfather, where she can work the land and have the freedom to sing hymns whenever she wants. She hides her government pension check, waiting for the right moment to slip out from under her son and daughter-in-law's watchful eyes. Her escape attempt is successful, as she manages to get back to Bountiful by the end of the story, though not entirely on her own terms.

Homing in to the parent-child theme established in earlier works, the script reveals immediately the central conflict in the play: the relationship between Mrs. Watts and her spiteful daughter-in-law as typically unpleasant. Foote's sympathies are clearly with Mrs. Watts, for he shows a reversal of roles: Jessie Mae in the "parent" role and Mrs. Watts treated as a child. Jessie Mae informs her mother-in-law that "This is my house and you'll do exactly as you're told," and orders Mrs. Watts to refrain from singing hymns in her presence since "hymn-singing makes [me] nervous." Instead, Jessie Mae plays the radio at all hours and fills her days with visits to the drugstore, beauty parlor, and picture show. As Mrs. Watts puts it later, Jessie Mae "thinks everybody's crazy that don't want to sit in the beauty parlor all day and drink coca-colas!" Her calling Mrs. Watts "Mother Watts" is clear indication that titles can be empty when void of true feeling, as Jessie Mae and Mrs. Watts could not be more estranged.

That Jessie Mae thinks of her mother-in-law as her disobedient child is particularly revealed when she and Ludie go looking for the runaway woman at the bus station. Venting her anger at Mrs. Watts on the nearest waiting passenger, Jessie Mae relates, "When people ask me why I don't have children, I tell them, 'I've got Ludie and Mrs. Watts—that's all the children I need!'" Her selfishness and impatience suggest the kind of mother she would be if she did have children.

Ludie does not share his wife's point of view, but as it is easier to let her have her way than to fight for control, he wavers between her and his mother, an ineffectual peacemaker. That he and Jessie Mae have no children is not a joking matter for him, though, as he openly envies his best friend, Billy Davis, for his three children. He unsuccessfully tries to cover his pain when Billy talks about his family: "I don't know if I could get along without my kids. I don't know how you get along, Ludie, what you work for?" That life is void of meaning for men without children is implied, if not Foote's major point.

While Jessie Mae could be viewed as the villain of the film, with Ludie as her accomplice, Foote cannot be accused of painting these characters any blacker than they deserve. Instead, he offers insight into their unhappiness, citing their childlessness as only one source of frustration. Living with one's mother-in-law has never been touted as a condition conducive to peaceful co-existence, and Foote, though he clearly sympathizes with Mrs. Watts, does not turn a blind eye to the difficult position in which she places both her son and his wife. Ludie's illness and the lack of money also add to the family's problems, eliciting the audience's understanding and acceptance of each of the three characters. This consistent generosity to all characters is particular to Foote's work and distinguishes it from most play writing.

In most of his scripts, Foote provides a contrast in characters to present his ideal relationship. In *The Trip to Bountiful*, this comparison is deduced when Mrs. Watts manages to slip away to the bus station and befriends on the bus to Harrison a young woman by the name of Thelma. Going back home to stay with her parents while her soldier/husband is overseas, Thelma tells Mrs. Watts, "I'm the only child and my parents and I are very close." Thelma's easy relationship with not only her own parents but with Mrs. Watts as well illustrates Foote's ideal mother-daughter union and expands the definition of family to include even the strangers one meets.

The need for such family ties for strength, love, and happiness is called to attention throughout Foote's work and especially in his description of Mrs. Watts. Thelma's appreciation of family and love of hymn-singing make her the perfect traveling companion, as well as the perfect daughter-figure, for Mrs. Watts. Just before the two part company, after Thelma has gone out of her way to take care of Mrs. Watts, the older woman tells her, "If my daughter had lived, I would have wanted her to be just like you." That her own daughter-in-law has not been this substitute daughter for Mrs. Watts stands in sharp relief against Mrs. Watts' new friend. As Mrs. Watts puts it somewhat wryly, "If your son marries you lose a son; if your daughter marries, you gain a son." Obviously, Mrs. Watts has neither daughter nor son, and her wish for Thelma to have been her daughter is as touching as it is telling of her situation.

Foote's depiction of the growing relationship between a "mother and daughter," as exhibited by Mrs. Watts and Thelma, also opens the discussion of unhappy unions between parents and children beyond that displayed by Jessie Mae and Mrs. Watts. When Thelma admits to loving her husband so much her friends think she is silly, Mrs. Watts is compelled to confide that she did not love her husband and that she could not "love anybody but Ray John Murray." When a bewildered Thelma asks why Mrs. Watts did not marry Ray John, Mrs. Watts spits out bitterly, "Because his papa and my papa didn't speak!" Crying even now, she explains how her father forced her to stop seeing the only man she ever loved.

While Foote's work often accentuates the unhappiness caused by thoughtless or manipulative parents, Mrs. Watts' situation in *The Trip to Bountiful* is the most poignant. As she continues to talk, she reveals more and more about her relationship with her domineering father, a man who strictly enforced his position as head of the chain of command in his family. But much as she resented his iron-fisted control over her life, Mrs. Watts obviously loved and respected her father, too. "My father was a good man in many ways," she insists. This sums up Mrs. Watts' opinion of all the authority figures in her life, including God, whom she associates with her strict father: she may not understand or agree with everything they impose upon her, but because she has been brought up to see herself as their subordinate, she will bow to their wishes.

Foote does not appear to pass judgement on either Mrs. Watts or her father for the roles they played in each other's lives. His depiction of manipulative parents in previous plays, however, would suggest disapproval of such attitudes, and Mrs. Watts clearly is portrayed as a pathetic victim in this scene. Still, Foote's work has never encouraged disrespect for authority figures, and it is his tendency to soften even the cruelest image by also alluding to that person's positive traits. The play offers no insight into Mr. Watts' motives for denying his daughter's marriage, so the audience is left to speculate about his reasoning, but Mrs. Watts goes on to reveal her appreciation for her father's protection of the birds around their farm and for the unmaterialistic value system he taught her. When the sheriff later admits he does not remember her father, Mrs. Watts is disappointed, though she realizes few people other than herself have memory of him.

In her revealed memories of her father, Mrs. Watts continues to draw connection between him and her view of God. The dialogue between her and the sheriff suggests Foote's awareness of the lack of spiritual concern in modern society. As David Neff writes in "Going Home to the Hidden God," "one suspects that Mrs. Watts' papa isn't the only father that is dead. As she talks about how her papa used to protect the scissortails and redbirds from hunters, we realize how closely her papa is identified with the heavenly Father whose 'eye is on the sparrow'" (31). While some viewers may overlook the underlying spiritual implications Neff takes for granted, his point is not without merit. Much of Foote's work lends itself to a spiritual interpretation, and *The Trip to Bountiful* makes this association clearest in this scene. To Mrs. Watts, both God and her parent are exacting fathers, but ones she respects and misses in her life.

It is interesting to note the association with the sheriff, Mrs. Watts' father, and God—all authority figures in her life. Though her father prevented her from marrying the only man she loved, she bowed to his will and even continued to love and respect him. She has no trouble accepting authority, conceding that "a rule is a rule," when the ticket taker at the bus station refuses to cash her check, and she has never minded suffering, even though she lost two of her three children early in life. "Understand me," she informs the sheriff and bus station attendant. "Suffering I don't mind. Suffering I understand." That in her eyes some of her trials have been caused by her father or other authority figures and some have been allowed by God demonstrates Mrs. Watts' tendency to combine all figures of authority, earthly or spiritual. But, because she has been brought up to be submissive to such figures, in spite of all her hardship, she has not complained. She even reasons that on days when it seems "the good Lord" is absent, He is not neglecting her but merely testing her appreciation of Him.

However, when Mrs. Watts discovers that Ludie and Jessie Mae have set the sheriff on her trail to prevent her homecoming, she does not hesitate to defy authority for the first time in her life. Vowing "no sheriff or king or president" is going to impede her intentions of returning to Bountiful, she insists the sheriff take her to her former home. Because she believes that her escape from Houston is evidence that "the good Lord is just with me today," Mrs. Watts feels she is being called home, by her father, earthly or otherwise, or by her home itself, and that is the higher authority, as far as she is concerned. Her persistence convinces the sheriff to take her out to the deserted town himself, for the sheriff, like the father and God she has known, can show compassion when it is needed.

Foote's depiction of the dilapidated farmhouse and the forgotten town Mrs. Watts discovers Bountiful has become is realistic, as is the old woman's disappointment in realizing her dream has dissipated. The scene suggests as well Foote's assessment of the sad state of affairs in modern society, spiritual or otherwise. Today, Foote intimates throughout *The Trip to Bountiful*, the mass of humanity has moved to man-made cities where the work is distressing and unfulfilling, leaving the farms—a possible source of peace—to grow up in weeds. But Foote's strongest point, as always, alludes to the necessity of maintaining family connections; his meaning is particularly evident when Mrs. Watts cries, "When you've lived longer than your house or your family, maybe you've lived long enough." Clearly, when one's purpose for living no longer includes one's family, one has outlived his or her time on this earth, Foote suggests in Mrs. Watts' outburst. However, when Ludie arrives and Mrs. Watts notices a resemblance between her son and her father, her spirits are bolstered by the evidence of her son's inheriting something from the man who was so important in their lives.

Ludie has attempted to forget this inheritance, as his life has failed to live up to his grandfather's example, though. When his mother asks if he remembers her father, he muses, "Not too well," recalling only his unfulfilled promise to name a son after him. But the hidden bitterness that he has no children explodes as he exposes the emptiness he suffers and the true reason he has tried so hard to forget. "Oh, Mama," he cries, "I lied to you. I do remember. I remember so much!" The regret caused by lack of family and the inability to perpetuate oneself reverberates throughout the scene, as Ludie alludes to his having nothing to work or live for, and thus, nothing to secure his future. His mother softens his disappointment, though, by pointing out that although they and man-made things are not immortal, God's creation will continue. "That's what I always took my strength from, Ludie," she explains. "Not from houses, not from people. . . . And it's given me strength once more . . . to go on and do what I have to do. I've found my dignity and my strength."

Foote admits in an interview with *Christianity Today* that he is "attracted to the sense of dignity in the human spirit that . . . allows [people] with grace to meet what comes their way and find the strength to survive." The "measure of dignity" that Mrs. Watts achieves though her physical and spiritual homecoming here is "as much as you can ask of life," Foote supposes. And, underscoring the spiritual implications of his work, he calls attention to "the fact that [these people's] religion must sustain them a great deal [as it] permeates their lives [and is] a part of their strength" (30). He illustrates this point in the former and following scenes.

To convince her son of the source of her peace, Mrs. Watts calls his attention to the cyclical pattern of nature with its promise of perpetual life, explaining, "We're part of all this. We left it, but we can never lose what it has given us." And Ludie, who became sickly and nervous only after he left Bountiful (and married Jessie Mae), answers, "I expect so, Mama." Proving that being reconciled with one's heritage has done him good, when Jessie Mae demands they hurry up, for the first time he has the courage to deal firmly with his wife and insist that they all try "to live together in peace."

Not only are homecoming and reconciliation possible, Foote's play implies, such experiences reap priceless benefits. Mrs. Watts demonstrates the positive effect her homecoming has had on her, too, as she agrees meekly to the new set of rules her daughter-in-law imposes on her for "running away."

This is more than just Mrs. Watts' usual acquiescence to authority; it is the reestablishing of peace of mind that her trip has brought about. As she kisses her petulant daughter-in-law on the cheek, Mrs. Watts explains, "I've had my trip. That's more than enough to keep me happy for the rest of my life."

Jessie Mae is the only one seemingly unaffected by the trip, and, pointedly, she is the only one who refuses to see Bountiful as the lost paradise. The only reason she accompanies Ludie is to satisfy herself that her mother-in-law's government check is safe, and the only reason she even gets out of the car when they get there is to speed Mrs. Watt's farewell to her homeplace along. When she scratches her best pair of shoes, she pouts, "I ought to have my head examined [for coming] out here to this old swamp!" The memory of another immature and dissatisfied character, Dixie in *Tender Mercies*, makes Foote's point through Jessie Mae even sharper.

Neff intimates that in Jessie Mae, "Foote offers . . . his vision of where the culture [today] is going" (30). For those who believe with her that hymns "are goin' out of style," replacing them with popular radio and "a picture show once or twice a week," understanding what Mrs. Watt's papa told her years ago, that "the world can't be bought," will prove difficult at best. It seems, then, that Foote's film holds the mirror up to modern movie-goers, calling them to come home, too, to a discarded source of peace that money cannot buy.

To solidify this final suggestion, when it looks as though Mrs. Watts is not going to be able to see Bountiful, though she has "come too far" to miss it, she warns, "Time is goin', time is goin'." As Cynthia Clawson sings the final verse of "Softly and Tenderly, Jesus is Calling" at the end of the film, it seems Mrs. Watts words are repeated, perhaps as an urgent invitation to the audience:

> Time is now fleeting, the moments are passing—
> Passing from you and from me.
> Shadows are gathering, death's night is coming:
> Coming for you and for me.
> Come home, come home. Ye who are weary come home.
> Earnestly, tenderly, Jesus is calling,
> Calling, oh, Sinner, come home.

With such explicit final words, Foote connects the physical homecoming with the spiritual, affirming his belief in the promise and benefits of familial reconciliation and making his religious point more loudly than ever before. And the final message seems to make its impact if, as Mike Grady writes in *Newsday*, "the film [has] a profound effect on people. At the end of the movie, people are apt to sit in silence, seemingly stunned, as the final credits roll past" (7).[9]

As has been established between Foote and his character of Mac Sledge in *Tender Mercies*, Edgerton draws a correlation between strong independent characters like Carrie Watts and Horton Foote himself, at least when it comes to insisting on doing film according to his own vision. He writes:

> There is little coincidence to the recurring pattern in Horton Foote's independent films where a number of key characters ultimately find peace and contentment by following their own way; and correspondingly, a series of others find themselves unhappy and regretful in hindsight for having ignored their better judgements. Carrie Watts, the central character in *The Trip to Bountiful* (1985), is in many ways the prototype of this preoccupation and motif in Foote's cinema because she embodies both impulses in one skin, having suffered for marrying a man she never loved, but then following her resolve to visit her family homestead in Bountiful, as her way of situating herself both psychologically and spiritually in the face of impending old age (8).

In that sense, then, Mrs. Watt's homecoming is Foote's homecoming; and as he travels, he takes Hollywood and its audience on a homeward-bound journey, too, suggesting there may be reconciliation for all.

Notes

Part I

1 *The Traveling Lady* was produced at The Playhouse in New York in October 1954, directed by Vincent Donahue and starring Kim Stanley in the title role.

2 *Baby the Rain Must Fall* stars Lee Remick as Georgette, Steve McQueen as Henry Thomas, and Don Murray as Slim. It was filmed in Waxahatchie, Texas, near Foote's hometown of Wharton; this may be one reason the film is a favorite of Foote's. "Oh, I love that one," he admitted in an interview. "I'm very proud of that . . . we did it in my hometown" (Wood, LFQ 228).

3 Stark Young, who wrote the introduction to the published play in 1955, has already called attention to this somber aspect of Foote's work, associating the "dark and hideous" elements of the play with Strindberg.

Part II

4 Foote submitted *The Chase* to a play writing contest in 1948 but was asked to withdraw the play from the competition by New York producer-director Herbert Schumland, who was serving as a judge for the contest, as he was interested in staging the play himself. Foote agreed to Schumland's proposal, but for unrevealed reasons, the play did not see production until April 1952, when it was produced and directed in New York by Jose Ferrer (Barr 47, 104).

5 The novel version of *The Chase* is written in short scenes, divided into sixty-six chapters, and into three sections entitled: "The Conspirators," "The Chase," and "The Exiles."

6 *The Chase*, the film, was released by Columbia in 1965; it starred Marlon Brando, as the sheriff; Robert Redford, as Bubber; and Jane Fonda, as Anna, Bubber's wife.

Part III

7 Robert Duvall won an Academy Award for Best Actor for his portrayal of Mac Sledge in *Tender Mercies*. The film also stars Tess Harper as Rosa Lee, with Betty Buckley as Dixie, Wilford Brimley as her manager, and

Ellen Barkin as Sue Ann. Bruce Beresford directed the film for Universal.

Part IV

8 Foote originally wrote *The Trip to Bountiful* as a teleplay for Fred Coe and NBC; it aired to rave reviews in March, 1953 and starred Lillian Gish as Mrs. Carrie Watts. A less successful three-act stage version ran thirty-nine performances in the fall of 1953 on Broadway, later being revived off-Broadway and in London. In 1985, Film Dallas I and Bountiful Film partners produced the adaptation at Robert Redford's Sundance Institute. The film was directed by Foote's cousin, Peter Masterson, who had been encouraged by Redford for several years to bring Foote's work to the screen (Hachem 40). Geraldine Page won an Academy Award for Best Actress in 1985 for portraying Mrs. Watts in the film version of *The Trip to Bountiful*. John Heard as Ludie, Carlin Glynn as Jessie Mae, and Rebecca de Mornay as Thelma are also featured. Foote produced the film with Sterling van Wagenen; it was filmed in Ellis County, Texas.

9 According to *U. S. News and World Report* (June 4, 1990), *The Trip to Bountiful* is one of the 1980's thirty-one top-grossing films based on stage plays, earning over $7.5 million in U. S. box office receipts alone.

Chapter Five

The Final Homecoming: The Orphans' Home Cycle

Between the unsatisfying experiences with Hollywood in the late 1960's and the rewarding success of the early 1980's, Foote spent a decade of semi-retirement in New Hampshire; he did not like "the direction theatre—or for that matter—America was going" (CBY 146). "The 1960's kind of crept up on me," Foote admits. "All of a sudden I realized all the changes [particularly in subject matter and coarse language in modern movies] were taking place" (Calio 76). Daughter Hallie, the actress who has portrayed her grandmother in the film versions of *The Orphans' Home*, has admitted, though, that the children were not so supportive of their father's career move. Remembering the tantrum she threw when told they would have to leave New York, Hallie also recalls it was the only time she has ever seen her father cry. "Please, just give me a chance," she remembers him petitioning his family. Now she is eager to add that she "admire[s] him as a writer" and likes "being his daughter" (Forsberg 21-22).

It was well into the 1970's when the last of Foote's four children had just moved out on her own, and he was feeling somewhat "family-hungry" (Hachem 40), that Foote drew the collection of nine plays together, taking only about a year to complete what he had mulled over in his mind for four or five. His parents had both died recently, and Foote recalls "that the writing of these [plays] was prompted by my thinking over my parents' lives and the world of the town that had surrounded them from birth to death" (Introduction xi).

Actually, since these plays were based on stories about his own father and family that he had heard all his life, the cycle was simply a mental homecoming of sorts. Still, he objects to the term "autobiographical" when discussing the cycle, as "they're not about me," he insists. "I think of them more as biographical in the sense that they are about my family" (Edgerton 10). *The Orphans' Home* cycle, Foote's tribute to his own background, brings his focus on the family and reconciliation between fathers and sons into the strongest spotlight of his career, providing a base for all Foote has written before and more clearly defining his predominant life-time theme.[1]

Perhaps more important in the long run is the contribution Foote's cycle makes to modern American drama. His creation of the nine united plays gives him the distinction of being the only American playwright to have written any collection of plays beyond a trilogy concerning one family of characters. What makes the cycle all the more interesting is that the complete collection sustains a single theme: the importance of family relations, particularly the bond between fathers and sons. The continuing of the familial theme connects *The Orphans' Home* cycle with Foote's entire canon, and though Foote realistically depicts his created community with all its negative characteristics, the cycle ultimately accentuates his firm belief in the need for and the hope of reconciliation.

The initial play in the collection, *Roots in a Parched Ground*, written in 1961, introduced Foote's father in the character of the eleven-year-old Horace Robedaux.[2] Set in 1890 in the "village" of Harrison, the story opens to reveal the boarding house that Horace's mother, separated from his dying, alcoholic father, is obliged to operate to support her family. When his mother decides to leave Harrison for Houston where she can make a better living, the boy determines to run away. "I'm going to hide out until Daddy gets well," he confides to his sister Beth Ruth, "and then I'm going to live with him. I'll work in the store and I'll read law and when I get grown, we'll practice law together" (30).

When Horace cannot be found in the ensuing storm, his mother leaves him to go on to Houston. His father dies that evening, and though his mother soon marries again, she is content to leave Horace virtually an orphan in the care of others in Harrison, rather than bring him to live with her and her new husband, who insists Horace must learn to support himself. Horace longs to be reunited with both his parents: "I want us all living together in one house" (41), he wishes futilely at the end. The pathos of Horace's situation illustrates the sympathy Foote has demonstrated with children who have become the victims of uncaring or absent parents, echoing the plight of many of Foote's young protagonists.

Foote extensively revised *Roots in a Parched Ground* when it was published along with the rest of the cycle in the late 1980's. Though the characters and situations are the same, with the emphasis on parent-child relationships intact, the material in the original play is used as background for the new scenes surrounding the death of Horace's father which have been added and take the spotlight. As this event was that which destroyed Horace's prospects of family, Foote focuses on it more explicitly to bring his father-son theme more clearly to the forefront of the discussion.[3]

Horace is twelve in the revised play, and his sister, whose name has been changed to Lily Dale, is ten; they have been living with their maternal grandparents, the Thorntons, because their mother, separated from their father, is already living in Houston and planning a second marriage. Their father, Paul Horace, once a brilliant lawyer, lies dying in the Robedaux home nearby.

Foote's interest in the father-son union engulfs this play as he demonstrates the kind of father Paul Horace would like to be if the circumstances were different. Horace's education is important to this well-educated man, and, although he is dying, he secures the word of his best friends that they will support his son in getting an education. The revised play supports Foote's view that children will respond favorably to this kind of fatherly interest. Wanting to emulate his father in everything, Horace is more determined than ever to get an education and become a lawyer after his father dies.

Although Foote does not elevate Horace's father to the position of his idea of the ideal parent, the love between the two seems to "cover a multitude of sins" in Foote's eyes. Similar to former works, Foote contrasts this loving relationship with the animosity Horace receives from his new step-father, Mr. Davenport. Making it clear he does not want Horace, Mr. Davenport believes a boy should quit school, learn a trade, and support himself, since that was what he had to do when he was growing up. That this attitude is directed solely at Horace underscores its harshness. Mr. Davenport has "fallen in love with Lily Dale" (63) and insists she live with them in Houston.

Foote also reveals the other side of the family coin in his depiction of Lily Dale and her estranged relationship with her father. Her opinion of Paul Horace has been shaped by the Thorntons' criticism, and she has sided with her mother in the separation. Having never developed an attachment for him, she refuses to look at her dying father and excuses herself from attending his funeral, convinced that if her parents are divorced, then he is no longer her father. She quickly gives her complete loyalty to her step-father, because if he "just worships her," then she is just as "crazy about him" (78). Although Paul Horace may have attempted a loving union with his son, there is little indication he has given his daughter equal time, and she has reciprocated his neglect. These two differing father-child relationships illustrate explicitly Foote's point concerning a child's reaction to parental affection: the one who is loved responds lovingly; the one who is not loved responds indifferently.

At first Horace is confused by the loss of one father and the almost immediate replacement of another. In scenes reminiscent of James Agee's Rufus in *A Death in the Family*, he goes about the community practically bragging about his father's death, receiving various reactions of sympathy. Foote uses this scene to highlight his theme of the impact the loss of a father can have on a child when Horace confronts the local drunk, Mr. Ritter. "It's terrible to lose a father," Ritter affirms, remembering that when he lost his, "Life was never the same again" (48). An obvious example of the failure a son may become without a father's influence or protection, Ritter's outcome serves as a sober warning for the now fatherless Horace.

Foote's play emphasizes the importance of a child's having a father-figure as a role model. With his father gone, Horace tries to fill the void with notions of the stepfather he has yet to meet, and he wonders if he should address the new man in his life as "daddy." When neither of his father's friends keeps his word about aiding Horace's education, Horace broaches the subject of living with his new family in Houston so he can go to school as he "promised my daddy" (81); his mother, however, informs him of Mr. Davenport's opposition. Realizing for the first time that he is unwanted, Horace tries to assume a nonchalant attitude with his friends:

LLOYD: Did you meet your new daddy? . . . What's his name?
HORACE: Pete.
LLOYD: What do you call him?
HORACE: Mr. Davenport.
LLOYD: Mr. Davenport?
HORACE: Yes.
LLOYD: I guess that's because you're not used to him. (Pause.) Do you think you'll ever call him anything else?
HORACE: Nope.
LLOYD: My mama says she bets you'll go live with them now.
HORACE: Nope. They want me to, but I won't go.
LLOYD: Why? I'd like to live in Houston.
HORACE: I wouldn't. They say if I do go, I'd have to go to school, and I'm through with school (83).

On his own and aware of his inability to keep his promise to his father, Horace lies to himself and his friend Lloyd, changing his purpose from getting an education to working in his uncle's plantation store to earn the money to purchase a tombstone for his father's grave. The Robedaux family is financially unable to bear the cost, and Horace has already learned that he cannot trust friends' vague promises to "get around to it one of these days" (87).

Foote is obviously sympathetic with all the children in the play who have been neglected by fathers in one way or another, especially those like Horace who have to mature before their time. Paul Horace's niece, Minnie, who claims to be "his favorite" (33) rather than his own daughter Lily Dale, has been deserted by her own father and seeks approval from her Uncle Horace. Foote's portrait of Paul Horace is balanced, showing him a loving and concerned father, but also a man who neglected his family because of his drinking. Lily Dale's seemingly unfeeling attitude toward her father is somewhat excused when looked at in this light, though Horace's continued loyalty to their father puts Horace in a more favorable light than any of the characters. Illustrating the importance of a father's influence on a child's life, Foote attempts to portray all characters fairly and compassionately, even softening Mr. Davenport's character by giving insight into his unhappy upbringing. He also demonstrates an understanding of the reality of being a father: good intentions cannot always be carried out, as fathers on earth are merely human.

Thus begins the cycle, labeled "a moral and spiritual journey of an orphan at the age of 12" (Sterritt 38), planting the early seeds of the need for father and family which take root, grow, and flourish in the other eight plays.[4] While Foote's detailed focus is specifically on Horace's family, his message concerning family unity and reconciliation is universal and clear.

Convicts, the second play in *The Orphans' Home* cycle, picks up directly where *Roots in a Parched Ground* leaves off and illustrates the hard life Horace is forced to lead now that his father is dead and his mother has abandoned him. It also calls attention to another of Foote's favorite topics, that of honoring the dead and maintaining connections with family, living or dead, as Horace has worked six months at his uncle's plantation store to earn the money to buy his father a tombstone. Surrounded by convicts and blacks who work the Gautier plantation and a drunken, mean boss, Mr. Soll Gautier, Horace must learn to fend for himself in this poor excuse for a home.

The play accentuates the need for a child to develop his own sense of worth. While the ideal situation would entail the child's receiving a positive self-image from the nurturing comforts of home, Foote realistically portrays the lack of such luxury in Horace's case and the reality of his having to create his own sense of well-being as best he can now that his parents have abandoned him. Because his life is void of any compassionate familial bonds, Horace tries to convince himself and those around him that his dead father loved him. Admitting, "my folks don't care what I do" (97), but needing to establish some loving connection in his life, Horace insists to Martha, the black cook, that "My daddy cared about me, but he's dead" (97). Whether Mr. Robedaux actually did care for his son or not, it is sad to realize that the source of the only love Horace can claim in his life is no longer there.

That lack of family concern is an unhappy and unnatural plight for a child is obvious even to the most hardened characters. The action in the play revolves around the murder of one convict by a another. When the killer is arrested and held at the store, even he questions why Horace does not live with his parents. His remarks support what Foote sees as inarguable: a child's place is with his family. *Convicts* also acknowledges spiritual implications cited in previous plays. When Horace attempts to say "The Lord's Prayer" for the dead convict, like many Foote characters, he has a hard time remembering the prayer in its entirety, once again calling attention to the dearth of spirituality in the lives of those who grow up without anyone to teach them moral values. That the murderer in the play is also the victim of a broken home himself underscores Foote's point about the negative influence of growing up without a father's guidance.

The play calls attention to the unnatural state created in the family by divorce and remarriage, as well as death, as the confusion Horace faced in the first play about having two fathers resurfaces in *Convicts*. Worrying about what will happen in heaven when his sister, who "calls her stepfather 'Daddy' . . . comes face to face with her real daddy" (118), the play implies that Horace has encouraged the distance initiated by Mr. Davenport out of loyalty to his dead father and because of his reluctance to replace one father with another. When Martha assures him the answers are "in the Bible somewhere," Horace can only hope they are somewhere; that things are not "by the book" is cause for concern, Foote suggests, and reason for his protagonist's confusion.

The significance of remembering one's family even when they are no longer around is highlighted in the play by Horace's tenacious desire to purchase his father's tombstone. He remains on the plantation, even though it is Christmas Eve, because his boss has not paid him the money earned for a down-payment on his father's monument. But even the inebriated Mr. Soll, who cannot remember who Horace is, recognizes the importance of this symbol of family devotion; he claims he has erected an expensive gravestone in his own father's memory and now insists on purchasing Horace's father's stone himself. Horace later realizes Mr. Soll has no intention of paying for the stone and that he even lied about the ostentatious monument on his own father's grave. Foote uses Mr. Soll to illustrate the poor father-figure Horace has had since his father's death and suggests his low opinion of such a man when he has Mr. Soll die that night in drunken delirium, with no "Christian funeral" to follow.

Convicts presents a bleak view of life *without* father, extending this image of destitution beyond the individual. At the play's end, Ben, Martha's husband, muses how the plantation will be neglected now that Mr. Soll is dead and the wilderness will take over once more. "The house will go, the store will go, the graves will go, those with tombstones and those without" (163), he remarks, calling attention to the inevitability of change, death, and decay in this life and the futility of trying to retard the passing of life by marking it with any sign of permanence. Horace, however, refuses to relinquish his dream, as the tombstone has become the symbol of his promise to his father and of the love he never had the chance to share, a symbol Foote has long honored.[5] The play does not relinquish, either, Foote's hold on the importance of the union between father and son that his plays consistently have illustrated.

The third segment in the sequence, *Lily Dale,* jumps to 1910, when Horace is twenty years old and employed as a clerk in a store in Glen Flora, a small community outside of Harrison. The play fleshes out more fully the uneasy relationship between Horace and his stepfather alluded to in the first two plays of the cycle. *Lily Dale* describes Horace's visiting his mother for the first time in years, in an attempt to reconnect with his family, while her husband is out of town visiting his own kin. When Mr. Davenport returns early, however, the old conflicts between him and Horace reach a climax, and in the end, Horace is, for all practical purposes, "fatherless" and on his own again.

Most of Foote's work examines the negative results of poor parent-child relationships, and *Lily Dale* exposes further the wounds caused by Mr. Davenport's unfeeling attitude toward his stepson. When Horace must ask his mother for return fare, Mr. Davenport upbraids him with, "Nobody ever gave me anything . . . What kind of man are you gonna make, taking money from a woman at your age?" (193) Later, when he learns of Horace's intention to find work in Houston to be near his mother, Mr. Davenport dares his stepson to ask for his help. "Nobody every helped me get a job" (202), he insists.

To be fair to all characters, Foote allows the audience to understand Mr. Davenport's resentment of his own unhappy past, but it does not excuse his inability to treat his stepson civilly as another human being, if not as a caring parent. For even though Mr Davenport remembers the pain of his own neglect, he does nothing to impede repeating it with Horace. His uncaring attitude stands as the strongest example of Foote's theme of the sad effects of an unfulfilled childhood, particularly when the victim has not learned from his past.

That such behavior only perpetuates further resentment is illustrated in Horace's reaction to Mr. Davenport's unkindness. Horace's hatred toward this man, who could have compensated for the loss of his father, becomes equally obvious. When an attack of the flu detains him as an unwanted and unwilling patient and Mr. Davenport unfairly accuses him of faking his illness to "get free room and board" (208), Horace explodes, letting the family know how much he despises his stepfather.

Though Foote describes both Horace and Mr. Davenport's backgrounds as cut from the same cloth, because of their jealousy for each other and their unyielding pride, their lives can never be stitched together. Foote uses this step-father/stepson example to foreshadow a similar attitude Horace will encounter in a future segment of the cycle when he meets the other man of significance in his life, his father-in-law, Mr. Henry Vaughn. Demonstrating how Mr. Davenport could and should have reacted to his stepson, though, Mr. Vaughn is willing to change and becomes the substitute father Horace has searched for all his life.

In contrast to Mr. Davenport's treatment of Horace is his lavish indulgence toward his stepdaughter, Lily Dale. Because

Horace's eighteen-year-old sister has become even more vain and silly than when she was a child due to her step-father's spoiling her to "make up for the daddy I never had" (177), as Lily Dale explains, the play demonstrates that when the loving familial bonds become excessive, they can be as damaging and unhealthy as the broken connection illustrated between Horace and Mr. Davenport.

Since their stepfather has withheld his affection from Horace, Horace cherishes the memory of his real father. Similarly, because of Mr. Davenport's attention, Lily Dale is not interested in remembering Mr. Robedaux. Foote's previously established point that a child responds to the treatment it receives from its parents could not be more clear. To balance Lily Dale's selfishness, he suggests that her attachment to Mr. Davenport may be her defense mechanism against the past, but her unwillingness to share her good fortune with her brother keeps this excuse for her behavior from being acceptable.

To illustrate, Lily Dale describes a recurring dream she has had of her brother's dying. In the dream her mother suggests burying Horace in the family plot in Houston, but Lily Dale snaps back, "'No we won't. I'll not have him buried with you and Mr. Davenport and me. I want him buried with his father where he belongs'" (236). Having secured a loving family setting in which she is the nucleus, she is too selfish and insecure to widen the circle to include her deprived brother who has asked her to share so very little.

In the end, Horace returns to "where he belongs," where he grew up and has recollections of his father, realizing he cannot compensate for the neglected years with the remnant of his family. Relying on distant cousins for support, he plans to return to Houston only to enroll in a business course and not to participate in a family that should have been, but is not his. Though Horace's situation does not reflect Foote's ideal family, the author portrays the reality of broken homes and their devastating results, while solidifying the audience's sympathy for his fatherless protagonist. Foote's stand on the value of loving family relationships could not be on more solid ground.

Foote allows the spiritual implications of his theme to resurface again at the end of *Lily Dale*, as well. On the train ride back to Harrison, Horace encounters Mrs. Coons, an outspoken Baptist woman he met on his trip into Houston. Having witnessed the state of his family, Horace realizes their problems are bigger than their ability to overcome, and though he has not been brought up to be religious, he seizes the only source of comfort being offered. Lacking an earthly father, Horace is forced to turn to a heavenly Father for help in undoing the mistakes of the past and present, as he asks that Mrs. Coons pray for the members of his family.

Foote implies, as he does in other plays, that the more specific the prayer, the more effective. When Mrs. Coons begins a general prayer, Horace interrupts: "My mother and my sister and me. Pray for *us*, Mrs. Coons, pray for *us*" (249, my emphasis). And while Mrs. Coons may appear a comical character, Foote is careful to portray her sincerity as she prays in the closing lines of the play to the "Father of mercy, Father of goodness, Father of forgiveness" (250) for each member of Horace's family. Implications of the connection between earthly fathers and God from earlier plays and the need to rely on a higher power are brought into clear focus at the end of *Lily Dale*. It is to Horace's credit that he still cares enough for his mother and sister to have them prayed for with him, even though they have met his attempt at reconciliation with reluctance and resistance. His attitude reflects Foote's toward his characters and his efforts to be generous even to the coldest of characters.

The fourth segment of *The Orphans' Home* cycle is *The Widow Claire*, set in Harrison in 1912, on the eve of twenty-two-year-old Horace's departure to Houston to enroll in business school. While this play has the least to offer in detailing Foote's journey into his family's past, it does maintain the parent-child theme, adding insight into the impact Horace's childhood has had and will have upon his life as an adult. A universal implication of Foote's family theme is demonstrated, also, by the depiction of the Widow Claire's fatherless children and their desire for a loving "daddy."

The twenty-eight-year-old Claire Ratliff, whose husband has been dead for about a year, has been on every single man's social calendar, and Horace is only one of her current callers. But although Claire is eager to enjoy life herself, she tries to think of her children, Buddy and Holly, first. Her deceased husband's dying words requested she marry again, because he wanted his "children to have a father as they're growing up" (312-313), and she is committed to considering each man she dates in this light. The children's need for a father emerges immediately in the play, calling attention to Foote's theme.

Exemplifying Foote's point, Horace has learned from his own deprivation that a father-figure is the most significant thing in a child's life; so, unlike most of Claire's gentleman callers, he does not mind the company of her two little children. Sympathizing with the little boy and girl, Horace allows them to put him in the role of "daddy" when he is at their house; Buddy even speculates that his father's clothes would have fit Horace, unconsciously verbalizing his desire that Horace take their father's place.

Of the other men Claire sees, her children like "Uncle" Ned the best, because, like Horace, he does not mind their company and promises to become a good father. A poignant illustration, Buddy cherishes Ned's picture, even taking it to bed with him, and both children hope their mother will marry Ned, instead of another of her beaux, the abusive and selfish Val Stanton. Unlike Horace's mother, who appears to have not even considered her children when remarrying, when Claire realizes what a poor stepfather Val would make, she decides "then and there to marry Ned, for their [the children's] sake" (328).

Horace, though dejected at the loss of Claire's company, agrees the marriage will be the best thing for her children; demonstrating a mature outlook bred by his own deprived childhood, he understands that the happiness and stability of one's children is more important than a grown man's pleasure. And while one family is reshaped with the promise of a happy future, unattached once more, Horace turns his thoughts to becoming a salesman and traveling the world. The world, after all, is the only home he knows, for as Marianne Moore put it in her "In Distrust of Merits" from which Foote took the title of his play cycle, "the world's an orphans' home."

The Widow Claire, looking at the fatherless family situation from the unique perspective of the half-orphaned children, Buddy and Holly, as well as that of the half-orphaned adult Horace, allows for even greater understanding of Foote's family theme than ever before. And because the Widow Claire's children are unrelated to Horace, the play broadens its meaning to include the outside family of the community, supporting the view that Foote's opus on his own personal heritage has universal value.

The first four plays of the cycle, then, not only introduce Foote's fictionalized family and community, but continue to illuminate his theme of the father-child relationship established in the earlier plays. Throughout the cycle Foote also maintains his charitable insight into his characters, an approach he has sustained in all his previous work. And while his depiction of the world has developed into a more realistic, sophisticated, and even darker perspective, he has not rejected the possibility of reconciliation for his characters in the end, as *The Widow Claire* and the rest of the cycle illustrate.

It was Foote's oldest daughter's suggestion that the family independently produce the plays with their own company, Cinecom International, that has brought three of the cycle to the screen already, with plans for the others.[6] The project has become a family affair for the Footes, with actress daughter Hallie taking the role of her grandmother (thinly fictionalized in the play cycle), and the other daughter Daisy helping costume the cast, while taking a small acting part. Son Horton, Jr., has accepted smaller supporting roles, while working as production and casting assistant. Wife Lillian, who has "never lost faith" in Foote or his dream (Freedman xiv), has handled most of the production work.[7] It is no wonder, then, that Foote is as "pro-family" as he claims to be (Hachem 40).

Hallie, whose leading role as Elizabeth Robedaux is one of the more important, has had the most to say publicly about the family project. Her "father's daughter," she loves her family and cherishes the opportunity for them all to work together. Hallie claims she gets along well with her father as the writer/director of the films, because "we see eye to eye on a lot of things." When she is acting, she adds, "I don't think of him as my father" (Forsberg 21). Her father agrees, admitting that he has learned how to retreat if and when their ideas concerning her acting conflict. As both a director and a father, Foote obviously knows what many of the fathers in his plays need to learn: how to demonstrate to one's children a father's love through a developed mutual respect.

Although at times, like most artists, Foote insists that his plays are purely fictional, created from his fertile imagination, Hallie is quick to point out that the characters in these plays are simply real-life portraits extracted from the Foote family album, some even complete with original names. She flatly states, "*The Orphans' Home* cycle is based on my grandfather and . . . playing my grandmother . . . seemed quite natural for me" (Personal letter 9/5/89).

Foote's success in achieving his purpose to entice the audience into making their own homecomings through their contact with his work is supported by his own daughter's response. Hallie reveals that she prepared for her role as Elizabeth by making a literal homecoming to Texas and using the objects she discovered in the family home (letters, clothes, and so on, that her grandmother had kept) as a "journal." Her homecoming became deeper and more significant, as she came to a fuller understanding of her own personal family background, while developing insight into her character. She writes, "Above all I felt very comfortable and often amazed at how similar my feelings in my 20's and hers in her 20's were. She became more like a sister or friend to me" (Personal letter 9/5/89). Her only regret has been that her grandmother did not live to see the plays; "I think she would have been pleased" (Forsberg 21-22) is Hallie's positive, if vague, assessment.

Nineteen-eighteen was the first play to be filmed, released in 1985 and followed by *On Valentine's Day* the next year. In 1987, PBS's American Playhouse produced the two again, for television, adding *Courtship* and putting the trio of plays in the proper chronological sequence under the blanket title *Story of a Marriage*.[8] To make the discussion of family reconciliation easier to understand, these three plays as films will be viewed here chronologically according to plot, rather than production. As the film versions follow the printed scripts closely, both will be discussed simultaneously, with marked differences mentioned as the need arises.[9]

The television production of *Courtship* closely follows the 1979 stage script; like many of Foote's previous plays, it focuses on the over-protective effects of a father's love on his children, suggesting the necessity of the child to reject the stifling relationship in order to grow as an adult. Mr. Henry Vaughn, one of the richest and most influential men in Harrison, controls his unmarried daughters just as rigidly as he controls his business affairs. Not understanding Elizabeth's or her younger sister Laura's "need to marry," Mr. Vaughn plans to be their sole provider, even beyond his death as he intends to leave them "the money to take care of them" (15).

Although Foote applauds the evidence of well-proportioned parental love in all his work, Mr. Vaughn's display of fatherly affection borders on the extreme, and *Courtship* accentuates the ill effects of such a stifling familial situation. When Laura protests to being an "old maid," her father squelches any independent thinking by telling her she does not know what she is talking about. Indeed, it is unlikely that she does, as her pitiful questions about life, sex, and death to her older sister demonstrate that Mr. Vaughn's authority has kept both girls in unhealthy ignorance.

The dangers of such ignorance and restrictions are illustrated further by the death of Sibyl Thomas, a neighborhood girl who "had to get married" and died in childbirth after trying to conceal her pregnancy "by corseting herself" (29). The Vaughn parents, however, view this local scandal as good reason to increase their control of their own daughters, using it as a lesson and adding myriads of warnings with family gossip of unhappy marriages. Mr. Vaughn even reminds Elizabeth of her own narrow escape with Syd Joplin, a former boyfriend she had hoped to marry.[10] He drives his point home:

> Remember Syd Jopkin. You said you could not live without him. . . . You were sobbing and crying so, I thought you would surely be sick. . . . Even your mother thought I had gone too far in my opposition and yet three days after he left here, it seemed to me you had forgotten all about him . . . You were glad I had prevented it. Weren't you? (28-30)

Foote suggests that such repression naturally leads to the child's defiance and further intimates that this rebellion may be the only alternative a child has in order to achieve an independent adult life. Although Mr. Vaughn thinks his lesson has sunk in, Elizabeth's rebellion runs unseen below her demure surface; for, despite her seeming acquiescence to her father's will, her mind is made up to defy her parents and elope with Horace Robedaux, with whom she has continued to correspond secretly. This first real challenge to her father's manipulation forces Elizabeth, like many of Foote's heroines, to choose between being "daddy's little girl" and becoming someone's wife.

Foote's message that deceit and rebellion of this type are the result of such unreasonable restraint in child-rearing could not be more clear, and this heavy authority of such father figures is common in many of Foote's family portraits. Even the forbidden marriage to which Mrs. Watts alludes in *The Trip to Bountiful* is repeated in *Courtship* in the tale of a maiden aunt. While Foote never denies the concern of such fathers for their children, their methods are questioned. As exemplified in the earlier play *The Old Beginning*, however, the child's initial breaking away from the father in order to become an adult is represented as necessary, so long as the reconciliation with the father is sought and attained before it is too late. Foote suggests, too, that children must try things their own way in order to appreciate more fully the father's role later.

Foote has described already the lack of affection Horace has experienced, particularly with his stepfather, Mr. Davenport. Mr. Davenport's inability to mature beyond his own bitter childhood has deprived his fatherless stepson a chance at a desirable relationship and has cheated himself out of the opportunity to fill his former familial void. Horace's encounter with Elizabeth's father threatens to become a repeat performance, for although the resemblance between Mr.

Vaughn and Horace Robedaux is obvious (both were orphaned as children and had to work hard to survive), Mr. Vaughn will not acknowledge the similarities. Though he grudgingly credits Horace for rising above his "miserable" background, he is afraid of allowing his daughter to become attached to such a battle-scarred victim of life and refuses to offer Horace the warmth and stability of the prestigious Vaughn family. Proving his willingness to grow, however, Mr. Vaughn eventually offers the kind hand of acceptance to his son-in-law, becoming more of an exemplary father-figure than Mr. Davenport.

This is the element focused upon in the next segments, "After the Elopement," and "Reconciliation," taken from the sixth play in the cycle, *On Valentine's Day*. It is Christmas Eve 1916, less than a year after Elizabeth has eloped with Horace, and the Vaughns have not forgiven the "children" for their defiance.[11] However, in the true spirit of Christmas, and because they have learned of Elizabeth's pregnancy and do not want to be estranged from the "future member of the family," they give in, coming over with gifts on Christmas morning to the rented room that serves as the Robedaux home. The spiritual implications of a baby's bringing reconciliation on Christmas Day need no further explanation in Foote's Southern protestant milieu.

It takes a mature set of parents to swallow injured pride in order to reestablish connections with rebellious children, but Foote underscores his approval of their growth in his depiction of the happiness of the restored family. This maturity exhibited by the Vaughns is highlighted further when contrasted with Horace's mother and stepfather. Although the Davenports had no objections to the elopement, neither do they have any desire to establish a relationship with the newlyweds. When Elizabeth confesses that Horace is hurt by his family's indifference, her father callously exclaims, "He should be used to it by now. He's never had a home." Mrs. Vaughn suggests he has a home now with Elizabeth, but her husband misses the deeper point, insisting a rented room in a boarding house can never be a real home. To him, home is "something that belongs to you" (80), just as his family is also something he possesses.

Foote does not intend that the audience view Mr. Vaughn as unfeeling or even materialistic. It is hard for a father who has nurtured his children to accept graciously the secondary position he himself must take when his daughter becomes a wife, and, presenting Mr. Vaughn in a sympathetic light, Foote demonstrates his understanding of the conflict such fathers must face. Still, Mr. Vaughn has difficulty completely relinquishing his parental role and his deeply entrenched desire to provide for his family, and he cannot resist offering to buy the couple a house, oblivious to Horace's need to purchase a home for his family himself.

Horace's having lived "like an orphan [in] more houses than he can remember," accentuates his desire to have his own home, but not one given him by his wife's father. Wanting to do the best thing for his new family, though, Horace acquiesces to Mr. Vaughn but insists the deed be in Elizabeth's name. Foote implies Mr. Vaughn's motives are pure, even if his ability to be diplomatic is questionable. To emphasize Foote's charity toward the character of Mr. Vaughn, Horace is shown to be appreciative of Mr. Vaughn's intentions of wanting to care for his children. Having grown up deprived of a father's providence, Horace envies Elizabeth and her brother "for having a father like that," and speculates, "If I'd had someone to help me like that, my life would be different" (82).

While *On Valentine's Day* focuses on the reconciliation between a father and his daughter and son-in-law, acknowledging the seeds for a positive family union that have been sown, it also portrays another reality: that sometimes a father's influence, providence, and advice can have little effect on some children. "Brother," Elizabeth's sibling whose drinking, gambling, and lying have led the Vaughns to despair, is a case in point. Impressed only by his father's bank account, Brother ignores the other values Mr. Vaughn had hoped to instill and seems unconcerned with pleasing his father. Foote suggests that Mr. Vaughn, who has tried to provide for his son's needs without spoiling him, is not to be blamed for Brother's behavior. While Mr. Vaughn may not have been the most approachable and understanding of fathers, Brother has to take responsibility for his own decisions and actions, as Foote implies that the relationship between a parent and child is a two-way street at which both need to work to make it a successful journey together. The next play, *1918*, illustrates this even more than *On Valentine's Day*.

Ironically, it is Mr. Vaughn's failure with his own son that leads him to appreciate his new son-in-law. Finally understanding the common bond they share are orphans, he comes to respect Horace and considers him more of a son to him than his own. "Poor Horace never had a father," he mourns. "[I] never had one, either, and now I have no son." He even acknowledges the peace and contentment that prevails in the couple's rented room is more valuable than all his wealth and security. "Things like that can't be bought" (102-103), he finally realizes, demonstrating he has learned a lesson or two from his daughter's defiance.

Foote's depiction of family relationships and the promise of reconciliation is stronger in *On Valentine's Day* than in any other play in the cycle. And because it is Foote's usual intention for his plays to show that the concern for family extends beyond the immediate kin, providing a rich background for his play are the members of the larger family, the Harrison community. All these characters seem to suffer from fragmented family relationships, but Foote presents each one as compassionately as he does realistically. These include the rather strange teenager Bessie, who seeks in Elizabeth the sister she does not have, and Miss Ruth, the "songbird of the South," who cries over the drunken Mr. Bobby Pate whose mother owns the boarding house in which she and Horace and Elizabeth live. Remembering how she sang "O Promise Me" at Elizabeth and Horace's wedding, Miss Ruth longs for a familial commitment herself and a home of her own.

Foote's point that the lack of an ideal father-figure in the home leads to negative results is borne out in the character of Mr. Bobby Pate. Wasting his aristocratic life drunkenly mourning his ex-wife's departure, he cannot remember his father, or that drinking killed him, too. He bangs his head against his bed when, like many Foote characters, he cannot recall his prayers, suggesting the dearth of spiritual stability in his life, and goes through the house, constantly looking for his mother, who like many single mothers in similar circumstances, has had to open their home to boarders. His final desire to have a family plot in the graveyard so that he and his mother can be "together even in death" is a futile, but common symbol of inevitable family reunion in Foote's work.

Sad as Mr. Bobby appears, Mr. George Tyler, Horace's cousin and one of his father's best friends, is even more pathetic, and even more exemplary of the need for familial reconciliation. Mr. George's mental condition is unstable at best, as he flits about the community, forgetting how to get to town, or, symbolically, how to get home or when to go to church. While Foote is not explicit as to the origin of Mr. George's derangement, the effects of unreconciled relationships and broken vows clearly suggest the root of the problem. Mr. George seems haunted by unkept promises made to Horace's dying father to "look after" his children (in *Roots in a Parched Ground*) and now tries to make up for his neglect by giving Horace $1,000.00.

Ignoring his own son Steve's attempts to subdue his erratic behavior, he convinces himself that Horace is the nonexistent son he had by Mary, Horace's aunt, whose heart he believes he broke by marrying her cousin. Similar to other Foote characters, Mr. George attempts a reconciliation with Mary by visiting her grave in Bandero. He stabs himself in the street after he is told there are no longer any trains making the trip, his son Steve trying desperately to reason with him. The most poignant scene of the film, and the one that most clearly illustrates Foote's theme on the need for reconciliation between a father and son, is Steve's lone vigil with his father's dead body, his weeping an inadequate attempt at communication with the father whose confusion led to the severing of the familial bonds.

The tragedy of the suicide is softened in the end by an explanation of death as one's homecoming to God, thus suggesting a spiritual element to the play that offers the hope of reconciliation to all.[12] This combination of the physical and the spiritual bridges *On Valentine's Day* with *1918*, the final episode of *Story of a Marriage* and the seventh play in *The Orphans' Home* cycle. Death resides with nearly every family in 1918, as the war in Europe trespasses into the womb-like Harrison, with casualties daily making the journey home to their final resting place.

Horace, thinking his status as husband and father protects him from serving his country, boasts that he would be "over there" if his family did not need him; his father-in-law, now accepting Horace as the son Brother has never been, attempts to help Horace achieve his desires by offering to take care of Horace's family so that his son-in-law can become a soldier. Appalled at the possibility of having to give up the security of his new-found family, Horace anguishes over losing favor with his father-in-law or losing time with his loved ones.

While it could be argued that Mr. Vaughn's offer to Horace is evidence of his inability to relinquish his fatherly authority, Foote reduces such criticism of Mr. Vaughn's manipulation by revealing his sincerely kind intentions. His wife explains, "He's always thinking of things for people he thinks they would like and then when they don't like it, . . . he gets his feelings hurt" (130). The influenza that sweeps like a plague through Harrison that year, however, saves Horace from having to make a decision, and the war is over by the time he recovers from his illness.

The establishment of new families when individuals separate themselves from their roles as children to take on new roles as parents themselves is the focus of *1918*, revealing a new element in Foote's family theme. The role of father has become the center of Horace's life; so the death of their only child is a major set-back to his recovery. Understanding how important establishing his own family tree is to Horace, Elizabeth buries their baby in the Robedaux family plot, even though her decision hurts her own parents. Accepting her role as a member of her husband's family, a mature Elizabeth sees herself as wife and mother now, rather than just her "daddy's little girl." Her determination to defy her loving, but domineering father in *Courtship* has yielded the proper fruit.

Foote is careful to ascertain that although children must break away from their former roles to establish lives and families of their own, the importance of maintaining all family connections is not diminished. Horace has exhibited his understanding of this point in his many attempts at reunion with his mother's family, and Elizabeth comes to realize this, too, when choosing names for their second child. Although she had considered naming the baby for her father, Elizabeth bows to Horace's desire to continue his family bloodline by naming the child for him, as Horace claims his mother "hurt his father deeply" when she named Horace for her father. The significance of remembering and honoring one's ancestors by passing their names down through the family line is highlighted, underscoring the value of the bond between family members and the creation of a true "chain of flesh" that links the past with the future.

Foote's plays not only suggest the importance of maintaining family unity, his writing about his family is a concrete demonstration of his theme. His utilization of the family graveyard in his works also serves as a physical symbol of his point. Horace's attempts to remain bonded to his father by paying him the final respect of erecting a tombstone on his unmarked grave so many years after his death add both poignant and comic elements to the theme. Not knowing "which grave is my father's," he questions everyone until he satisfies himself with its location and purchases an expensive marker which he has "planted" on the grave. All the loose ends of the father-son relationship are finally tied together, rendering Horace a peace from the reconciliation that he has never known before. However, when Horace proudly points out the headstone to Mrs. Boone, his peace is shattered by her observation that the tombstone is on the wrong grave. Horace's ability to see the humor in the situation is indicative of his realization that the bond with his father has survived without the aid of this concrete symbol all these years, and it is not necessary now.

Several of the works previously discussed have lent themselves to spiritual interpretation, and *1918* opens itself to this possibility, acknowledging the role religion plays in the lives of Foote's characters. The play intimates that "prayer meetings in all the churches" may have been responsible for

Harrison's deliverance from the modern plague of influenza, as the tide of death turns following the community's collective prayer. Mr. Vaughn, not an overly religious man himself, also admits Horace's "life was spared by the Lord" (147). The connection between earthly fathers and God suggested in earlier works again surfaces in *1918* when Brother's problems, cited in *On Valentine's Day*, come to a head in this film. Rather than take responsibility for his own misdeeds, he excuses his shortcomings, blaming them on the frustration that has developed from his strained relationship with his father: "Be like Papa! Be a fine, good Christian man like Papa!" he explodes. "I ain't never gonna be like Papa in a million years. I'm no damn good!" The god-like pedestal his father occupies seems as unattainable as heaven to the boy who has no desire to be anything but wealthy and to get rich the easy way at that. And Elizabeth's reaction to her brother's state of affairs when he asks her for money to pay for a former girlfriend's abortion further solidifies this connection between their demanding father and their view of God. "Oh, my Father," she gasps. "Oh, heavenly Father! . . . Papa is going to be furious" (133-135).

Realizing he could be a "father" himself, Brother begs his sister to "never tell Papa or Mama," but when she writes out the check to cover his misdeeds, Brother's anguish dissipates immediately. Here Foote adds another dimension to his discussion of fathers and families: the ability to physically become a father and the maturity it takes to live up to that responsibility are two different things. Brother, while proving he is capable of the first, has learned no more about the second than he knew before his careless mistakes.

Only when Mr. Vaughn ships Brother off to work on a cotton boat does the prodigal Brother appreciate the good home and parents he has left. The opening song, "Keep the Home Fires Burning," which underscored the soldiers' desire to come home from the war in Europe, now broadens to include Brother's war with himself; just as Harrison welcomed the returning soldiers with parades and speeches, however, so Brother is insured of an equal homecoming when his battle is finished. Thus, Foote reiterates his belief in the promise of reconciliation, in spite of the problems his characters have had to handle throughout the cycle.

When a son is born to Horace and Elizabeth later in the film, (the fictionalized Horton Foote, Jr., himself) (Edgerton 10), the real meaning of cycle is defined and the example of life renewing itself in spite of death strengthens *1918*'s positive conclusion. Widening the scene to include the outside family of Harrison, Mrs. Boone adopts an orphan boy after her son Clay dies. The negative aspects of living with a woman like Mrs. Boone, whose attitude resembles Miss Kate's in *Baby the Rain Must Fall*, does not diminish the optimistic tone Foote establishes at the end of *1918*. The closing song of the play is equally significant as Miss Ruth and Elizabeth join in singing a hymn that emphatically states Foote's theme of homecoming, both earthly and spiritually: "Oh, the peace of God be near us./Fill within our hearts Thy home./With Thy bright appearing cheer us./In Thy blessed freedom come./. . . Fill within our hearts Thy home" (176-177).

Thus the theme of father-child reconciliation binds the three works *Courtship*, *On Valentine's Day*, and *1918* together just as it ties them with the rest of the plays in the cycle. Perhaps more appropriately, *Story of a Marriage* should have been labeled *Story of a Family*, as it details the lives of each family member rather than just Horace and Elizabeth's, but the difference is slight. More important, these three from *The Orphans' Home* cycle not only bring the characters home, but Horton Foote, and the rest of his family by their involvement in the project, makes his own homecoming to the land and heritage of his people, revitalizing the bond that obviously exists with a father he obviously cherished.

The last two plays in *The Orphans' Home*, *Cousins* and *The Death of Papa*, were the last to be published, in 1989. The title of the eighth segment in the collection aptly sums up Foote's focus on the family, as all the characters in this play feel compelled at one time or another to discuss kinfolks, for good or ill. Old vendettas, especially those over misplaced inheritances, are renewed, as the true meaning of kinship and family is misunderstood.[13]

Foote also includes in his examination of family the human tendency to let greed or pride blur the focus on what is truly valuable in family relationships. Horace has not allowed his past to be a drawback in his establishing and maintaining family connections. Owning his own business in 1925, the thirty-five-year-old father of two has demonstrated his understanding of what family means by giving his Cousin Gordon a position as clerk with him; Horace empathizes with Gordon's struggle to get an education since his own father has died. Horace has always "stuck by his kin," even his own mother and sister who did little to make him feel wanted. In *Cousins*, when his mother faces surgery, Horace forgoes operating his store on its busiest day to go to Houston to be with her and even endures having to associate with his stepfather.

The "message" of many of Foote's plays seems to be, "Love thy neighbor," but in *The Orphans' Home* plays, the directive is more likely to be "Love thy family." *Cousins* suggests that the latter commandment may be harder to keep than the first. This is particularly apparent in Horace's dealings with his stepfather. The unfairness of Mr. Davenport's attitude toward his stepson, detailed in previous plays, is brought to even greater light in this play. Cousin's Gordon's observation concerning how he and Horace address Mr. Davenport is adequate illustration:

> GORDON: I like Cousin Pete, although he doesn't have a great deal to say. . . . I call him "Cousin Pete," although he's my uncle by marriage. What do you call him?
> HORACE: Mr. Davenport.
> GORDON: What do your children call him?
> HORACE: Uncle Pete.
> GORDON (laughing): Uncle Pete? They call him Uncle Pete and he's their stepgrandfather. And you call him Mr. Davenport and he's your stepfather and I call him Cousin Pete and he's my uncle by marriage (7).

That Horace has been treated as distant kin by his own stepfather is obviously a slight Horace has never been able to overcome, and the partiality both Horace's mother and stepfather have shown to his sister Lily Dale adds insult to his injury.

It is to Horace's credit that he does not despise his mother; that he is the "hero" of *The Orphans' Home* cycle clearly illustrates Foote's philosophy about maintaining family connections at all costs. Truly heroic in overcoming his deprived childhood, Horace is presented as the ideal family member in Foote's collection. His unwillingness to lie, however, when his mother tries to get him to assuage her guilt is demonstrative of Foote's unrelenting adherence to reality. Horace admits that the only relatives who have "always been good to me" (40) are on the Robedaux side of his family; his declaration is not intended necessarily as a criticism of his mother, but simply as the acknowledgement of the truth.

Although there can be no question that Foote's sympathy throughout *The Orphans' Home* cycle has been with Horace, in his usual compassionate way, he fairly demonstrates in *Cousins* that the mother should be excused, at least in part, for her actions. When Corella awakens from surgery, her delirium reveals how her repressed past has haunted her, giving insight into the role she has played. Mistaking her son for his drunken father, she voices the burden she has carried: "I just can't bear it, Horace . . . to have the children see you this way. I'm taking them home to Papa. He said I could come home and bring my children home. He said I would always have a roof over my head as long as he lived" (73). Here, Foote calls attention again to those women who have to shoulder both parental roles when their husbands do not accept their rightful responsibilities for their families.

"A family is a remarkable thing, isn't it?" Cousin Minnie remarks to Horace, her favorite cousin. "You belong. And then you don't. It passes you by. Unless you start a family of your own" (91-92). That Horace has filled the holes in his family himself by adding new members to it in his wife and children seems to be Foote's advice to all who are suffering from the absence of loved ones: if one is without family (relying on the double entendre for the word "without": lacking relatives and being left *out* of one's family, that is), one must attempt to create caring kinfolks, as Horace Robedaux has done. Horace attributes his belief in family and his newfound happiness to Elizabeth's love and acceptance.

Cousin Minnie mentions, too, the most inescapable and inevitable fact of human life: "so many [of the relatives] are dead." And another cousin, Lewis, drives this point further home, expanding the boundaries of family to include the entire community, when he remarks: "Cousins . . . a lot of them dead, you know. The graveyard is full of our cousins. The town is full of them. We'll be in that graveyard someday. . . . Why, the graveyard will be full of cousins" (99).

But in the proper family unit, Foote insists, when one dies, it should not follow that the dead one is forgotten. Elizabeth demonstrates this philosophy as she remembers their first child, Jenny, who died in *1918*. In typical Foote fashion, she plans to decorate Jenny's grave with flowers. "I don't forget her," she affirms. "It's like Mama says, you think of her differently than the others, but you think of her" (90). Foote, agreeing with his character, writes in the introduction to his first four plays, "Many of us do care . . . and we do care to remember, and we give to our children and their children our versions of what has gone before" (xiv). Foote's writing about his ancestors in *The Orphans' Home* cycle is proof that he thinks of them, and in recreating them through the written word, he has given them extended life.

Samuel Freedman's interview with Foote for the New York *Times Magazine* has been reprinted as an introduction to the published collection of *Cousins* and *The Death of Papa*. "*The Orphans' Home* cycle," Freedman writes, "starts in 1902 with the death of Horace Robedaux's father and ends in 1928 with the death of Elizabeth's, each event shattering a family." The introduction goes on to include Foote's recollections of that dreadful experience that reshaped the lives of his family and dictated the direction his career would take years later:

> "The event that always stuck with me, the event I've always been groping toward as a writer, was the day my grandfather died," Foote says. "Until then, life was just magic. I never felt so secure in my life . . . knowing . . . my grandfather was the most respected man in town. . . . I think it [his grandfather's death] was the turning point to my whole family. He was kind of a king. And from then on, we had many problems that he would've shielded us from. He was just such a symbol" (Freedman xvii-xviii).

Much of *The Death of Papa*, the final play in the Cycle, is told from the perspective of Horace, Jr., Horace and Elizabeth's son who was born at the end of *1918*. An inquisitive youngster, young Horace seeks to satisfy his insatiable desire to know all that is going on in his family by first listening to all the adults have to say, even when they would prefer he did not, and then asking questions to explain what he does not understand. Freedman describes him as "quite clearly, a writer in the making" (xiii).

That this ten-year-old child is the thinly disguised author himself is particularly obvious when Foote describes himself in words that echo his characterization of the young Horace, Jr.: "'When I was growing up,' Foote says, 'I spent half of my time in the house listening. I always loved old people . . . [and] could sit and listen for hours. . . . I always wanted to go back for more'" (xx). It is through these bouts of listening that both Foote and his re-created "alter ego" piece together the story of the grandfather's death and the impact it has on not only the family but also the entire community.

In the play, Elizabeth expresses pity for her child for having been subjected to the family stories over and over. "Poor boy," she sighs, "he's heard it enough. He's sick of hearing about it, I'm sure" (166). But Elizabeth could not be more wrong in her final assessment. Both Foote and his character delight in family gossip, fact and fiction. And though the character's grandmother cautions him not to repeat everything he hears, her words are lost on the potential "recorder" of his family's past.

Centering once more on the father-child theme established so firmly in the preceding plays, *The Death of Papa* portrays the day of his grandfather's death, exactly as Foote remembers it. The devastating impact a father's death can have on his children, a topic much of Foote's work has explored, is revealed immediately, as, upon the discovery of Mr. Vaughn's death, a heartbroken Elizabeth runs to embrace little Horace, crying, "Son! What are we going to do? What are any of us going to do? . . . Dear God! Dear God! Help us all" (105). Though she defied him to marry Horace, she always loved her father and depended on the security his wealth and position provided.

She maintains her strength by leaning on her sympathetic husband, whose entire life has been shaped by the death of his own father.

Mrs. Vaughn, stricken with grief, is not unlike a daughter herself who has lost the father she had thought would shelter her always from the realities of life. "Oh, my God!" she exclaims, "Henry tended to everything ever since we were married. I feel so helpless!" (126) Because she feels "nearer to him out there" (122), Mrs. Vaughn makes continual trips to the cemetery. Her plans to erect a large headstone in the family plot echo her son-in-law's symbolic action for his father, but her wealth allows for her also to finance a stained-glass window "in the new church in his memory" (144). This gesture of remembrance symbolically links the image most of Harrison had of Mr. Vaughn with a spiritual fatherly figure. But Mr. Vaughn's death reduces the elevated image the man may have had of himself as almighty provider and protector and shatters the family's fantasy that the powerful Mr. Vaughn might even live forever.

Mr. Vaughn's death seems to hit the perpetually inebriated Brother the hardest of all. His mother, however, tries to justify his excessive drinking, suggesting it comes from grief. "After all," she reminds Elizabeth, "he's lost a father that he loved, just like you have" (132). Wanting desperately to believe in her son, Mrs. Vaughn puts Brother "in charge of it all" (132), and having never earned his father's approval when he was alive, Brother intends to redeem himself by taking his father's place. The challenge proves too much, though, as Brother squanders his father's fortune, mishandles the property and crops, and eventually lands in jail for killing a man in a drunken brawl. He initially excuses his inability to live up to his father's standards with: "The ghost of Papa is heavy on me. I get so sick of people saying, 'I know you're going to turn into a fine man like your papa. Henry Vaughn's son couldn't help but be a fine businessman.' . . . I'm stupid. I've no judgement" (155).

Brother continues to justify himself by blaming his father for occupying too high a pedestal for him to attain. "I'm sick to death of hearing about how Papa did things," he rants.

"Was he so perfect? Was he some kind of god? I didn't think he was so damn perfect. I thought he made plenty of mistakes." Brother goes on to admit his intimidation of his father: "I was scared as hell of him," he confesses. "He always made me feel like I couldn't do anything." Claiming, "I'm never going to be Papa," he insists, "I don't want to be him, or like him in any way" (157).

The dangers of parents expecting much from their children without guiding them along the way are implied by Brother's ravings, as one can clearly see through his diatribe against his father to the insecure and unfulfilled son Brother has always been. While Mr. Vaughn may have demanded more than Brother was able to give, however, a review of Mr. Vaughn's attempts at leadership with his son reduces the seriousness of Brother's charge against his father. That Brother really did love and respect his father and desired a closer relationship with him is demonstrated later in his apology to his mother. "I worshiped my father," he now wants her to know, and owning up to the cause behind his weakness, Brother admits his drinking stems from knowing that "I can never in any way live up to him. Not in any way be worthy of him" (159).

Foote allows the contrast between Brother and Horace, seen by Mr. Vaughn himself in earlier plays of the Cycle, to reveal itself. When placed in a similar position as Brother, at an even earlier age and without Brother's concerned relatives and money, Horace dug in his heels and got to work. For these reasons, Horace is the only person who comes close to being worthy of Mr. Vaughn in Mrs. Vaughn's estimate. When she seeks his advice now that Brother has disappointed her, Horace agrees that "when I got into trouble there was no one I could turn to to help me out." But when his mother-in-law wonders if that is the best approach, as all their methods have failed with Brother, in all honesty Horace has to add, "there was a time I felt very bitter about it. I felt no one cared about me at all" (181).

Though the drawbacks of a privileged upbringing are suggested by Brother's failures, Foote refuses to support the other extreme illustrated by Horace's deprived background, either, despite this character's encouraging outcome. While it may appear Foote is offering a lesson in "damned if you do, damned if you don't" child-rearing, his point is not so complicated. Most would agree that nurturing a child with a parent's love is preferable to excessive indulgence. Perhaps many parents err to some extent in this respect, and the fathers and mothers in *The Orphans' Home* plays are no exception. The healthy balance of discipline and love, hard work and security is Foote's recipe for child-rearing and for the establishment of stable, happy homes.

Although Foote does not imply that Brother's outcome was his parents' fault, he contrasts their approach with the more successful methods of his own father (in the character of Horace Robedaux). Horace, Sr., determined not to make the same mistakes with his son that the Vaughns did with Brother, plans to instill in his son the importance of hard work and discipline. That love and encouragement temper these lessons is Foote's directive for secure family relationships, as Horace assures his son, "I'm going to stand by you in any way I can and I'm going to see you get an education if you want one. I don't want you ever to have to scratch around the way I have" (163).

Included in the education Horace has in mind for his son is a detailed study of their family history; having learned how to become a successful adult and parent from his own uneven past, Horace realizes how important it is that Horace, Jr., be deeply rooted in his heritage. Little Horace attempts to remember all the stories told him about all the generations of fathers in his family, and young though he is, he begins early to honor the practice of visiting the graves of his deceased family members in order to maintain those memories that are his inheritance. Having heard Gertrude, one of their black servants, express a desire "to help my people," Horace, Jr. decides that this is his ambition. "I'd like to help my race, too," he tells his mother. "What can I do?" She advises him to start by being a good man like his father and his grandfathers before him.

As the connections between the character, little Horace, Jr., and the writer, Horton Foote, become obvious to the audience, it is easy to see that Foote has honored his particular people by remembering them through his writing and recording the details of their living for posterity. He has continued, also, the presentation of his views on the importance of good family relationships for secure homes and a stable society, offered through his consistently compassionate depiction of realistic characters.

Notes

1 The cycle was completed, but filming was interrupted so that *Tender Mercies* could be produced in the early 1980's.

2 Foote wrote *Roots in a Parched Ground* as a teleplay for the Dupont Show of the Week; it aired in 1961 under the title of *Night of the Storm*.

3 The time of the play is changed from 1890 in the original *Roots in a Parched Ground* to 1902-1903 in the revised version, bringing the setting closer to the actual dates of Foote's father's life (Personal communication 7/28/89).

4 *Convicts, Lily Dale, The Widow Claire, Courtship, On Valentine's Day, 1918, Cousins,* and *The Death of Papa* chronologically fill out the rest of the sequence, ending with the death of Foote's maternal grandfather in 1928.

5 *Convicts,* starring Robert Duvall, is in the process of being filmed and is due out November, 1990.

6 Herbert Berghof, of HB Playwrights Foundation in New York City, produced *Courtship* (1978), *1918* (1979), and *On Valentine's Day* (1980), under Foote's direction. Staged readings off-Broadway of The *Widow Claire* were presented in 1982. Later, in 1986-87, *The Widow Claire* and *Lily Dale* enjoyed off-Broadway productions. The Widow Claire was included, also, in *The Best Plays of 1986-1987*. Since the filming of *Courtship, 1918,* and *On Valentine's Day,* many of the Cycle plays have been produced throughout the United States. (See Gerald Wood's "Chronology" in *Selected One-Act Plays of Horton Foote,* pp. xxiii-xxviii.)

7 Only son Walter, a lawyer in New York City, has been uninvolved thus far in the family collaboration in filming the plays from *The Orphans' Home* cycle.

8 *Story of a Marriage* featured the following cast: Hallie Foote as Elizabeth Robedaux, William Converse-Roberts as Horace, Michael Higgins as Mr. Henry Vaughn, Rochelle Oliver as Mrs. Vaughn, Matthew Broderick as Brother Vaughn, Amanda Plummer as Laura Vaughn, Horton Foote, Jr., as Steve Tyler (in *Courtship* and *On Valentine's Day*) and as Jessie (in *1918*), Daisy Foote as Ally (in *Courtship* only), Carol Goodheart as Miss Ruth, Jeanne McCarthy as Bessie, Richard Jenkins as Mr. Bobby, Steven Hill as Mr. George Tyler. Ken Harrison directed *On Valentine's Day* and *1918*; Howard Cummings directed *Courtship*.

9 Because Wharton, the Footes' hometown, has changed too much from the way Foote remembers it as a boy, *The Orphans' Home* cycle films have been shot in nearby Waxahatchie, Texas, where *Tender Mercies* was also filmed, and in Brookhaven, Mississippi.

10 This affair is the focal point of the earlier play, *Flight*. In that work, however, the girl actually marries the boy against her parents' wishes, only to be deserted by him in the end. Foote adds in a recent interview, "*Flight* and *Courtship* are about the same story, only done differently. Actually it is my mother's story . . . but she never married the man" (Wood, LFQ 235).

11 *On Valentine's Day* was renamed simply *Valentine's Day* in the 1987 Grove Press edition. Although the film title indicates it is Christmas *1916*, Elizabeth tells Mr. Bobby it is 1917 and that they are "at war." Later in the film when it is Easter, Elizabeth says again that it is 1917, and that she and Horace have been married one year that past Valentine's Day. Obviously, she is wrong when she says it is 1917 and that they are at war at the beginning of the film. The film *1918* takes place a year later, covering only that year. Foote has admitting to confusing the dates, claiming he does not keep track of details of that nature very well (Personal communication 7/28/89).

12 The explanation of death as one's homecoming to God is illustrated by a story Elizabeth relates from her childhood. She reveals going to look for her dead sister's grave when she was a child, remembering how she pointed out to Mr. Billy Lee, a friend of her father's, that Jenny was in the grave. When he corrected her that her sister was not there, Elizabeth recalls asking, "Then how did she get out of there?" Mr. Billy Lee then assured her that "God took her home with him," thus reinforcing the awareness of the ultimate home with the ultimate Father.

13 The practice of kin-placing is apparently one in which Foote himself has been personally involved most of his life; "I'm in touch with six or seven generations living in Wharton" (Wood, LFQ 227), he announces proudly, though his connecting with family members surely is not so superficial as the characters he depicts in *Cousins*.

Chapter Six

The Later One-Acts: A Darker Vision

The eight remaining plays in Gerald Wood's collection of Foote's one-acts, along with two other unpublished plays to be discussed in this chapter, were written in the 1980's and are illustrative of a darker vision of American society. While Foote does not seem to have abandoned his former view that a well-knit family can overcome most of life's hardships, he seems more aware that fewer families in current society bask in such secure and loving relationships. The bitterness and confusion of the lives of the characters in these later plays make Foote's acknowledgement of the necessity for healthy father-child relationships in families all the more poignant and urgent.

The lack of such emotional wealth in these plays, along with the overabundance of rootlessness and hopelessness, speaks clearly of what Foote sees as the basic cause of the present crisis in the American home. Many of these last plays also suggest a spiritual famine in modern society as the core of this family crisis. While Foote does not ignore what he sees as a disappointing reality, neither does he waver from what he sees as a possible promising solution, although his allusions to these conclusions are often subtle. This reference to the spiritual is one of the unique contributions Foote's plays have made in American theatre.

The Man Who Climbed Pecan Trees, first produced in 1982, "is Foote's darkest short play to that time," Wood writes in his introduction, "because, written after the disorder of the sixties, it reflects the breakdown of the traditional social contracts that the playwright observed during that troubled decade.... With the loss of an authentic and nurturing sense of history, friendship, community and the family order become threatened" (266). Wood concludes, "re-acquiring a sense of tradition, a home to live in, is the deepest need in this play" (267). *The Man Who Climbed Pecan Trees* also provides the most explicit illustration of a family's relying on a father to the point of crippling their ability ever to stand alone.[1] Previous plays have demonstrated the devastating effects of an absent or misguided father on the family, but the helplessness of the characters in this play results in a hopelessness unequalled in the early works.

Set in Harrison in 1938, *The Man Who Climbed Pecan Trees* portrays the Campbell family which has been trying unsuccessfully to cope with life ever since the father died. Mrs. Campbell recalls that death prevented her husband's plan to provide homes for each of the children to live in, and the lives of his children have crumbled when they have been forced to stand on their own. The eldest son, Brother, cannot forgive himself for losing their father's insurance money in a dishonest business deal; and the youngest son, Stanley, a heavy drinker since his father died, has taken to climbing the pecan trees in the courthouse square when inebriated, making himself the laughing stock of the neighborhood.

Mrs. Campbell admonishes Stanley to quit drinking lest his son discover his father's weakness, but the child is not naive about his father's condition; he asks his mother, "What is Daddy doing outside . . . ? Is he drunk again?" (282) Modern children possess a clearer understanding early of their world, the play suggests, and since Stanley has not been able to emulate the father he adored, this early wisdom may be the result of these children not having had the same privilege of such protective fathers. Having little control over his behavior, Stanley longs to return to the time when his father was still alive to guide him; he begs his brothers for advice, but they also cannot take the place of their father. The play implies that all the children are ignorant of successful living since their father is gone. Stanley turns to his mother for help, but she is little solace, for even though they are still sitting in "the house Daddy built for us all" (288), they are no closer to solving their problems than they were before. Stanley cries out that he is falling, although his mother is holding him tightly, futilely, in her arms.

What strikes the audience most forcefully is the condition of the family after the father is no longer around to keep it in order. The physical houses he built for his children cannot sustain the life he tried to instill in them when he was alive, and all his plans for his sons to "be real boys" (280) seem to have died with him, as the boys cannot seem to manage on their own. This may seem to be another perspective on manipulative parents as depicted in many of the earlier plays. When parents try to order the lives of their children, some rebel and go their own way, as such early plays as *Only the Heart* and *The Old Beginning* demonstrate; others may acquiesce to such parental control, as seen in *Tears of My Sister*, for example. In *The Man Who Climbed the Pecan Trees*, however, there is little evidence that Mr Campbell was an overbearing or thoughtless father; he is portrayed, instead, as a generous and concerned man. This play poses the question: when the parents are no longer there to answer questions, what happens to the children, crippled now by inexperience in running their own lives? Unlike *Death of the Old Man*, in which the helpless Rosa is rescued by an outside agent and old values are restored, the "children" in this later play can rely on no such *deus ex machina*, for none arrives nor is there any indication of future arrivals. *The Man Who Climbed Pecan Trees* demonstrates that Foote's perception of the world as a large, caring community has changed since his early plays.

While *The Man Who Climbed Pecan Trees* simply may present a realistic exhibition of a single broken family, the play may well serve also as a symbolic picture of the lack of spiritual values in current society. The following scene suggests such an interpretation: when Mrs. Campbell recalls Stanley's childhood explanation as to why he climbed trees, his reply was, "Trying to get to heaven" (286). While it may have been a joke at the time, now that he has returned to his childhood activity as a drunken adult, however, the illustration takes on definite spiritual significance, as the family believes their father is now in heaven. Stanley's attempt to reach his father in heaven may be simply a mistaken drunken antic to reestablish contact with the source of his childhood security. It may also serve, however, as a Babel-like symbol of modern man's unsuccessful reach for divine connection in an aspiritual society.

It may be significant that the preacher Stanley visits for help is not at home, implying Foote's subtly voiced commentary on modern society's spiritual state. The early plays suggest that "God's in his heaven, all's right with the world." These later plays intimate that if God is in his heaven, there is little communication between him and his creation, for the world could not be in a worse state. And while Foote continues to portray all characters sympathetically—Stanley is to be pitied, not ridiculed, for example—Foote cannot, in the name of realism, portray them as successful or fulfilled individuals.

Foote's *The One-Armed Man*, produced in 1985, is the most unusual of all his work, bearing little resemblance to many of the plays previously discussed.[2] This work encourages the interpretation of its action as a commentary on the state of the family in modern society, as its depiction of a man's search for his lost arm becomes a symbolic search for personal and spiritual connections. Wood agrees, writing in his introduction that "*The One-Armed Man* ends as almost pure psychological and symbolic theatre" (415). Ned McHenry, having lost an arm while on the job at the cotton gin, also has lost his position, for his manager C. W. Rowe refuses to keep a crippled employee on the payroll. Thereafter, McHenry haunts Rowe's office, steadily demanding the return of his arm. Finally, he invades Rowe's office with a pistol and shoots the older man.

The play suggests a father-son relationship between the two men that has soured when the father-figure has valued his business over his "son's" welfare. When the "son" suspects his "father" is either uninterested in his needs or unable to fulfill them, McHenry reacts desperately. Rowe tries to pacify him with "Son, be reasonable," but an offended McHenry warns, "Don't call me son" (425). Any father-son relationship that may have had the chance to exist between the two men is impossible now that the father-figure has let down the "son," and the exchange becomes a singular symbol of the failed family where materialism has replaced compassion and care for the individual.

As in other works, Foote sketches in Rowe's personal history, softening somewhat his unsympathetic image. Wood sees the boss not so much as "evil," but as "an unwitting agent of . . . social decay" (416). Rowe's "humanness," however, cannot compensate for the irrevocable damage he has allowed and the lack of concern he displays. The play shows Rowe trying to reason with McHenry by foolishly comparing McHenry's tragedy with his own son's less important loss of a toe during the war. "He don't let it get him down" (426), Rowe brags, hoping to persuade McHenry to a similar attitude. But like a child angered when compared with a sibling, McHenry is not soothed by the analogy.

"Foote has imagined a time when command has replaced compassion, when force and control have replaced love" (416), Wood explains. That the play exhibits a religious sign of the times is also suggested. Foote uses the following scene to illustrate his previously suggested point about the lack of spirituality in today's world. Before McHenry shoots his boss, he forces the older man to get down on his knees and pray. Rowe confuses "The Lord's Prayer" with a childhood bedtime verse, exhibiting his lack of spiritual as well as human understanding; in his entanglement, McHenry shoots him and turns the gun on Pinky, the office assistant, insisting that he, too, recite the prayer. Pinky's stuttering is little different from his boss', however, revealing a similar spiritual emptiness and predicting a similar end for him, as well:

McHenry: Pray . . .
Pinky: Yes sir. (A pause.) How in the hell does it go? My God, how does it go? You killed him. . . . I'm gonna pray. I'll think of something. Our Father . . . which art in heaven. Our Father. Hallowed be thy name. Our Father. . . . (428).

The lights fade as the weeping Pinky inanely repeats "Our Father," while McHenry remains over him with the gun. Pinky's rusty attempts to communicate with his "heavenly Father" are as unpromising as the likelihood of Stanley's reaching heaven in *The Man Who Climbed Pecan Trees*.

While Rowe and Pinky's confusion certainly may result in part from their fear, it is significant that McHenry insists they *pray*, rather than merely plead, for their lives. Equally important is the prayer that he requires they recite is one any Christian should be able to voice, especially one who claims to "teach the men's Bible class at the Baptist church," as Rowe does. Rowe has boasted also of contributing to the church where he is a deacon and choir member; therefore, *The One-Armed Man* serves as an illustration of Foote's criticism of hypocrisy among church-goers. The outward display of religion cannot atone for the absence of compassion for one's neighbor, the work suggests.

Moreover, while it may be argued that McHenry is deranged and, therefore, a poor spokesman for Foote's point, the script does not depict McHenry as crazy, in spite of what seems to be an insane request for the return of his arm. The play makes it clear that the audience is to sympathize more with McHenry than with Pinky or Rowe, particularly when the latter man is shown joking about McHenry's condition and offering him Russian hats and Coca-Colas to compensate for his loss. Foote compassionately presents his one-armed man as a victim who reacts desperately when his demands for restitution are ignored.

Wood is correct in citing that while "the social issues are less hidden in the fabric" of this play, it "should not be read as a political allegory" (416). Obviously, Foote's play has illustrated how technical progress has cost a hefty fee with the expense of man's health and safety; however, as in all Foote plays, the realistically presented characters draw our attention to themselves and away from any blatant agit-prop message their predicaments may suggest. The focus on prayer at the end, however, suggests Foote's deeper interest in spiritual concerns and implies his belief that the crux of society's problems are more spiritual than political. Wood agrees, calling *The One-Armed Man* "more religious, even visionary, than . . . political" (416). The breakdown between generations and the disintegration of the caring community in favor of prosperous business advancement are obvious, particularly when viewed from the angle of the father-son relationship. But the significance goes deeper, as Foote guides us to view the characters and their situation through a spiritual lens, apparent when McHenry requires his victims literally to pray for their lives.

The connection between earthly and spiritual fathers is established through the discussion of sons and fathers and the meaningless repetition at the end of the play of "Our Father." Foote implies that the destruction of the earthly relationship and the emptiness that exists between physical fathers and sons may be also the visible expression of the invisible, the concrete demonstration of the abstract reality. Either a lack of spiritual depth has eroded personal relationships or the growing greed that has gobbled up the concern for family has escalated to a spiritual blindness. Foote does not engage himself in the argument, however; he simply presents society's current situation as he sees it. The readiness with which Foote's work lends itself to spiritual interpretation of a kind characteristic of the Protestant South distinguishes his works from the bulk of American play writing.

The Roads to Home, a trilogy of plays Foote revised and presented in 1982, is set in Houston in 1924.[3] Again, both Foote's spiritual impressions and his portrayal of the impact of fathers on their children are highlighted. Annie Gayle Long is introduced in the first play of the trilogy, *A Nightingale*, as a pathetic young woman who is losing touch with reality, forgetting she is a married mother and running away one minute and then remembering her family and trying to care for them the next. She spends most of her time in this play in disjointed conversation with Mabel Votaugh and Vonnie Hayhurt, two older women who try to comfort and reason with her.

The deep bond between children and their fathers and the tragic results when that bond is severed has been alluded to in other Foote plays; it is illustrated explicitly in *The Roads to Home* as the cause for Annie's mental breakdown. She recounts a childhood event that has haunted her ever since its occurrence: being with her father when he was gunned down in front of his bank. This subject continually resurfaces in her confused conversation, revealing its effect on her mental condition. While it would be unrealistic to reduce the impact witnessing a murder is sure to have had on the child, the event also supports Foote's intimation that a child's relationship with its father has lasting effects into its adulthood, as well.

The Roads to Home leads its discussion from the earthly into the spiritual realm, as well, when Annie insists that had she known how to pray, her father would be alive still. She explains to her friends:

> I went to him [her father] lying on the pavement. Miss Rosa Gilbert came up to me and she said to pray like you've never prayed before. "I don't know how to pray," I said. "Get down on your knees," she said, "and Jesus will tell you what to say." "He's bleeding," I said. "Call a doctor." "Pray," she said. She held me and she began to pray out loud and Papa was bleeding and people came running from everywhere then. Dr. White, Dr. Burton and Dr. Ellroy. And they stood looking at him and Miss Rosa was praying and Dr. Ellroy said, "You can stop your praying now, Rosa, he's dead." And he was. He was dead (302).

Annie begs her friends to teach her to pray, but when Mabel and Vonnie encourage her merely to memorize "The Lord's Prayer," Annie questions the reason behind this lesson. Mabel explains, "Because when you know that and someone says you should pray, you can just repeat that. Now—'Our Father which art in heaven. Hallowed be thy name . . .'" (305). While Mabel's advice might have saved Rowe in *The One-Armed Man*, Annie rejects her instruction by pointing her finger, shaped like a gun, at Mabel and childishly shouting, "Pow. Pow. Pow. Pow" (305). Obviously, at the mention of "our Father" in the prayer, she thinks of her own father and how he was killed, implying Foote's father/Father connections. For Annie, whose father and Father are apparently both dead to her, the chance for her to straighten out her tangled life is slim. Unfortunately, her friends provide little assistance.

Wood explains the situation in his introduction: "Though there is genuine hunger in the play for a system of beliefs and values that would give direction and meaning to the characters' lives," he writes, "for many, like Vonnie and Mabel, easy literalism and the public display of religion are more important than a genuine sense of compassion" (292). The play supports this philosophy that Foote's work (*The One-Armed Man*, for example) has championed before: loving one's neighbor and bearing one another's burdens are of greater value than outward religiosity. Annie illustrates this intimation when she rejects the ladies' offer to recite the prayer, with "I don't need prayer. Thank you. I need to be mature and self-reliant, a doctor told me. I need tenderness and mercy" (312). While praying "The Lord's Prayer" sincerely is not the object of criticism here, the substitute of mindless ritual in place of concern for others' needs is highly suspect in Foote's eyes.

Even the mentally unstable Annie realizes that a mindless incantation of words cannot overpower life's tragedies, for although true prayer might accommodate Annie's needs for strength, rote memorization without any understanding cannot serve as a placebo for problems of such magnitude as Annie's. They are also too great for her feeble attempts at maturity and self-reliance, as the last play of the trilogy, *Spring Dance*, reveals Annie in a mental institution. As she sits with other patients in the nursing home (a pathetic excuse for a real home), Annie's conversation reveals she is no further down the road to recovery than she was in the first play. This breakdown of family, with little hope of speedy reunion, prevents any hopeful conclusion and makes the title, *The Roads to Home*, all the more ironic.

The second play of the trilogy, *The Dearest of Friends*, focuses on the equally empty, though less tragic, lives of Mabel and Vonnie, Annie Gayle's comforters in the first play. In need of comfort herself, Vonnie confesses to Mabel that her husband has developed a romantic attraction for another woman. Immediately the question of the role of spirituality arises as Vonnie worries that her lack of real religious involvement has something to do with the emptiness in her life and marriage. Although "born [a Baptist and] expect[ing] to die one" (303), as she once joked, now Vonnie muses, "I can't help wondering what my life would be like if we'd stayed home and gone to church" (329).

Just as often as Foote's work seems to point an accusing finger at the secular community for its lack of Christian charity, it does not flinch from exposing the hypocrisy of the so-called religious. As in *The One-Armed Man*, Foote's criticism sounds loudly in *The Dearest of Friends*, especially when it is revealed that the "other woman" is "a churchgoer [who has] always acted so pious" (335); the women also discuss other church members who have had affairs. The point Foote has made previously that an outward show of religion is no substitute for true spirituality is clearly supported in this trilogy.

As always, Foote's charity toward his characters extends even to the straying husband, Eddie, who is depicted more as unsure than unfaithful. Eddie admits his own confusion, spiritual and otherwise, when he joins the friends at their house later that evening. "I've tried to live right all my life, to be good and do the right thing." That these superficial steps may not lead to peace and contentment is a revelation that Foote's characters are just beginning to comprehend. Although she does not express exactly what her prayers are, Vonnie announces in the end that "if prayer does any good, he'll get over it. I pray night and day that he does. . . . And God usually answers my prayers. So I'm just going to keep on praying and I know He won't let me down this time" (343).

Vonnie seems to have learned from her marriage crisis that to meet the needs of both her physical and spiritual life, she must replace outward religiosity with sincere prayer. If it is Foote's point that such prayer is more effective and indicative of one's spirituality, as other plays support this supposition, the change in Vonnie's prayer life is encouraging sign of her growth. That *The Dearest of Friends* comes in the middle of the trilogy, followed by the less hopeful *Spring Dance*, however, leads one to speculate more pessimistically on the overall well-being of these characters. Perhaps, Foote is creating a realistic balance with the summation of the three plays: as in the actual world, some people's lives improve, others do not.

The Prisoner's Song, along with *Blind Date* and *The One-Armed Man* (both already discussed), was presented under the collective title *Harrison, Texas*, in 1985.[4] More than either of the other two plays in the collection, *The Prisoner's Song* dwells on the relationship between fathers and their children, particularly the grief one experiences when the other one dies. Here, Foote repeats his view from such plays as *Ludie Brooks* on the futility of excessive attachments to the dead and the necessity to overcome such sorrow through generosity to one's community.

John and Mae Murray, who married against her father's wishes, are facing bankruptcy because John has been unable to find a job. While this situation may link *The Prisoner's Song* with earlier Foote plays exemplifying "father knows best," here John has reformed from his drinking problem, the source of his father-in-law's disapproval, and he longs for the day when her father will "be man enough to . . . say, 'I owe you an apology. I was wrong about you. You're a fine man'" (398). The importance of a father's approval is evident in this play, as the affirmation from his father-in-law keeps his mind occupied throughout the play as he goes from one prospect of employment to another.

John's opportunity for a job in the oil fields lies with the wealthy Mr. Luther Wright, but Mr. Wright cannot bring himself to relinquish the memory of his dead daughter, Mary Martha, long enough to establish any real and lasting business deals with John. He even insists the Murrays visit her grave with him where he has erected an ostentatious tombstone, and he repeatedly requests that Mae sing his daughter's favorite song, "The Prisoner's Song," as he sits a prisoner to the song and to his undying memory of his beloved daughter.

While Foote uses Mr. Wright's condition as an illustration of the excessive father-child relationship, he also demonstrates another point dear to his heart through this character: the realization that loving, human connections are more important than business ones. Unlike John, who still believes his fulfillment lies in the accumulation of wealth, Mr. Wright has come to realize the emptiness of a full bank account when his family is incomplete. He confesses to Mae:

> When Mary Martha died I said to my wife, "Mama . . . they can take everything I have. My oil wells, my cotton, my cattle, if they will just give us back Mary Martha." . . . A man with three daughters came up to me the other day and said, "How come you are so rich and I hardly have a dime?" and I said, "How come you have three daughters and mine was taken from me?" Well, that stopped him. "That's something to think about," he said (404).

Mr. Wright can do nothing else but think about it, questioning whether his daughter's death is a punishment from God for his indifference to religion and allowing a beautiful memory of a father-daughter relationship to fester into an unhealing wound of grief and pain. While Foote surely approves of maintaining family remembrances—he has dedicated his writing life to such a cause—his portrayal of Mr. Wright clearly demonstrates the need for moderation and endurance to conquer maudlin self-pity. Here, not only is Mr. Wright entrapped in a stagnant existence, but his ability to help others through his wealth and connections also is impeded. Unlike the doctor in *The Rocking Chair*, who dedicated his life to his community after his daughter died, Mr. Wright's role as a father-figure in his community-family has been suffocated by his selfish sorrow.

The title of the next play, *The Road to the Graveyard*, evokes images of Foote's attraction to family cemeteries. It also is illustrative of the adherence to reality in this writer's works, as all roads ultimately lead to the graveyard. In this play, Foote suggests that the exchange of family stability for the endless search for prosperity hastens the journey. Like many others, this play is also an explicit portrayal of the crippling effects on children when overbearing parents refuse them the chance to lead lives of their own.

In his introduction, Gerry Wood writes, "*The Road to the Graveyard*, like many of Foote's plays, is about the family in transition. . . . Once the regenerative cycle of the family order is broken, the center will not hold" (430).[5] Set in Harrison in 1939, the action takes place in what was once "a fine, well-built, one-story house" (432) that has degenerated into an overall unkempt state, an immediate symbol of the demise of the family, as well. The play opens to reveal spinster daughter, India Hall, who has given her life to care for her ailing parents. Her best friend, Lydia Darst, shares her predicament, as she also has sacrificed herself to care for aging parents. Less resigned to her task than India, she complains about her burden to her admiring, less courageous friend and accuses both their parents of mishandling the rearing of their children:

> What I want to know is what was wrong with you all? . . . You and Mama and Papa and Miss Lillie. Whatever was in your minds? (She is screaming now.) Why didn't you drive us out of the house and make us learn something to support ourselves by? . . . Who's gonna take care of me when they're gone? Nobody. Who's gonna take care of India and myself after all our years of service to our families? (438-439)

However, there is no easy solution at this late stage, and Lydia can only console herself and India with the feeble platitude, "Well, we can sleep in peace nights. We've stood by our parents" (456-457).

While Foote does not condemn children's seeing to the welfare of their aging parents, he does criticize such misplaced parental priorities. Allowing daughters to sacrifice their lives for the sake of their parents is not training them "in the way [they] should go" (Proverbs 22:6). And despite India's difficult role as caregiver, her parents continue to treat her as a child, demanding her respect, even when their behavior is childish, and criticizing her for having no social life which their demands have restricted.

Continuing the lesson that this kind of childrearing does not guarantee a child's love for its parents, *The Road to the Graveyard* also presents the two sons who have demonstrated their appreciation for their family by moving away and ignoring them. Sonny, the brother remaining at home who "always had respect for our [parents'] wishes" (446), has grown up without ambition, clearly a product of his unsuccessful upbringing. Moreover, his mother reminds him that it will be his duty after the parents are gone to look after India. "Sister deserves to be taken care of" (451), his mother has the audacity to admit.

The inanity of the world created by the parents in *The Road to the Graveyard* culminates in the play's ending where the family is revealed sitting aimlessly on the porch, the "children's" catching imaginary rabbits for their mother a lasting impression of the fantasy world this misdirected family has created. And although Foote has continued to draw his characters sympathetically, demonstrating pity rather than ridicule or judgement, he has illustrated how even family-oriented homes can result in crazy-houses when the proper methods and motivations of upbringing are twisted and ignored.

The final play in Wood's collection of one-acts, *The Land of the Astronauts* (1988), is Foote's latest (to date), and its portrayal of Harrison is the most contemporary.[6] Set in Harrison in 1983, during its role as a "bedroom town" (467) for people who work in Houston, *The Land of the Astronauts* is, in Wood's opinion, "a present-tense play about the false idols of our times" (461). Lack of values and misplaced responsibilities have led to the breakdown of the family this play illustrates.

A subplot in *The Land of the Astronauts* introduces several families whose father figures have ruined their lives, causing their children to pay for their parents' irresponsibility. The overall negative effect of the subplot is indicative of Foote's view of the condition of the family in modern society when parents have neglected their responsibilities and children have been required to shoulder both their roles, as well. The depiction of the main characters in the play is no more encouraging, though, and supports much of what Foote has already said in previous plays about the difficulties in being the "perfect" father.

Phil Massey has worked hard to maintain his duties as father and husband, but, like Will in *The Oil Well*, his priorities have become confused and misdirected. Fascinated by the Space Program in nearby Houston, Phil vows he would "give twenty-five years off his life to be [an astronaut]." He dreams of living on the moon and predicts that since Catholics, women, and blacks have been allowed in the Space Program, "maybe the next thing is that they will send up a family . . . A father, a mother, and a little girl. And that would be us" (493), he promises his daughter. Phil's including the family in his list of minorities implies that the "ideal" family may be in the minority in today's society and brings Foote's portrait of the state of the family in modern society into clear and immediate focus.

Phil's obsession with becoming an astronaut has culminated in his leaving Harrison to find work in Houston near his heroes. When he fails to send for his family, his wife reports him missing; the police in nearby Baytown indicate they are holding a man who claims he is "an astronaut that had lost his way" (487). When his wife Lorena arrives to get him, Phil tries to explain his confused situation: working hard to provide for his family has not resulted in the kind of life he desired. "Why can't I go up into space and leave this earth and all its troubles and frustrations behind?," he cries, "Why can't I be an astronaut? They are human beings, aren't they? Just like me. . . . I work and work and get nowhere and I'm tired" (497).

Foote's depiction of this character is sympathetic: the man has labored to provide for his family, but he cannot seem to advance. Part of his argument is reasonable: if the astronauts really are "just as plain as you and me," then why should not any ordinary person aspire to their position? But on a deeper level, when Phil claims to be an astronaut who has lost his way, the symbolism is obvious: ordinary man, astronauts and restaurant waiters alike, are all seeking for a better life than their society or this present world can offer, and in their searching, they have become lost, tired, and confused. While it could be argued that Foote is making a socio-political observation, the following equation of Phil's paradise with heaven suggests a more spiritual statement in line with previous Foote illustrations.

Phil supports this symbolic theory with his description of "the land of the astronauts":

> The land of the astronauts will be beautiful, of course, not like here. A beauty we have never seen before and perhaps can't even imagine, and the people living there . . . will be happy all the time. Day and night. They will have no petty cares, no worries. They will have abundance all around them. They will be good and noble and kind. . . . The land of the astronauts is peaceful and there are no cares and worries (506).

Like any well-meaning father, Phil longs to present such a life to his loved ones; here, he is painfully aware of his failure to achieve this paradise on his own or provide it for his family, but he holds fast to his belief that someday his children or their children will attain his vision. While Phil's imaginings are little different from the description of any utopia, one cannot help hearing the echoes of any number of Christian hymns describing heaven. That this is Foote's intention is apparent, as during the play it is his written direction that "a program of hymns" (494) be played on the radio and that certain characters hum "religious songs" (506) in the background. Furthermore, when Phil's daughter shares her father's dreams with her homeroom teacher, the teacher admits Phil's vision sounds "more like heaven to her" (483).

As the deputy, Buster, takes Lorena to Baytown to get her husband, he plays hymns on the radio, informing his passenger that he is "going with a girl that is very religious. I never have been," he admits, "so I'm trying to catch up" (494). Later, Buster suggests that Phil "try religion" as the answer to his problems. "I'm trying it," he confirms. "My fiancee says it will bring me peace of mind" (500). Although Phil remains silent, Buster's advice does not ring hollowly through the scene. In the entire play, he is the only character who seems to have his life together; the sheriff introduces him to Lorena as "the level-headed one around here. Nothing gets him upset," adding "if anybody can settle it, [he] can" (466). Foote, avoiding an overt religious statement, seems to speak more loudly on this subject through his characters than he ever has before. As it is Foote's latest play, it may serve as a definitive statement on his father/Father theme.

The Habitation of Dragons, although written and produced in workshop in 1986 before *The Land of the Astronauts*, is the last of Foote's plays to receive public recognition.[7] Like *The Land of the Astronauts*, it introduces more complex characters than the early plays employed, characters who have had to deal with similar problems in this modern society. But like nearly all the previous works, it too reveals character motivations steeped in the complications of father-child relationships. Set in Harrison in the present, it also makes a strong comment on the necessity of forgiveness within the family.

Briefly, Leonard and George Payne, once very close brothers after the death of their father, become estranged when Leonard fires George from their law firm and supports his brother-in-law Billy against George in the County Attorney election. Bitter when Billy wins the election, George manages to build up a respectable law practice on his own. Billy discovers that his sister, Leonard's wife, Margaret is having an affair with Wally Smith and shoots him; in the meantime, Leonard's two boys accidentally drown.

Given a suspended sentence for his crime, Billy leaves Harrison to start a new life in Houston. Leonard and Margaret face a bitter separation, but she finally persuades her husband to stay with her to help heal the wounds they have all suffered. A humbled man, Leonard reaches out to reestablish the bond with his brother, as well, who has taken over Billy's office and kept Leonard's business afloat during the crisis. Although tragedy has struck, lives have been untimely taken, and trusts have been shattered, the play ends with the promise of reconciliation.

What makes *Habitation of Dragons* of particular interest to this study is the motivations of major characters, which, once again, are rooted in father-child relationships. More complex than in previous plays, the background to these connections requires close examination. Although the younger George does not remember their father very well, Leonard carries with him very significant memories. Their mother, Mrs. Payne, remembers that Leonard and "his father were inseparable," though when their father was supposedly killed in a hunting accident, for once, Leonard was not with him. The doctor, however, informed Leonard that "if he'd gone he might have . . . save[d] his father's life," and Mrs. Payne recalls that "when Leonard heard that, he grieved so he took sick, and . . . has never gone hunting or fishing again" (16).

Leonard later reveals that he has lied about his father's death all along, informing the family that he found the suicide note in his father's coat pocket. "That's why I took sick," he explains, "and I couldn't tell anybody what I'd found. . . . For a long time after that," Leonard continues, "I was so ashamed of him and what he'd done that I couldn't stand to hear him even talked about" (77). When others had thought he was too grief-stricken to speak of his father, he was actually too embarrassed and angry. Burdened with the secret shame and grief of his father's suicide, Leonard worked hard to replace his father in their family and to compensate for the reduced income on which the father's death forced the family to live.

Leonard has had to deal with the disillusioning discovery that the father he admired was actually cowardly and weak. While most children discover their parents are not perfect sometime during their lives, Leonard has had to bear the truth about his father on his own. Moreover, he has had to become his father's substitute in the family he abandoned. Such unnatural responsibilities for a son to carry naturally take their toll, and Foote's point about the influence of the father on the son is well-supported here. Determined that his young sons not experience a financial burden like the one he knew growing up, Leonard has become a "workaholic," leaving little quality time for his children whom he loves. And though they love their father, the boys prefer his friend Wally Smith, as he always has time for them. Their mother has turned to Wally, too, for the affection and attention she has not received from her absent husband. Leonard's commitment to maintaining his father's role has cost him the very relationship he desires with his wife and sons.

When the boys drown and the affair comes to light, Leonard blames it all on their "whorish" mother: "It's for her sins my boys were killed. Their death is her punishment" (55), he accuses, ignoring his own role in the tragedy. Foote suggests that Leonard's guilt from being unable to save his boys has led him to deny his responsibility. Helpless and heartbroken by his sons' death, he feels the need to blame someone other than himself. Margaret also believes that the boys were taken as retribution for her adultery, and she screams hysterically to her absent children, "your Mama is sorry. Please, please forgive your Mama" (56).

This obsession with punishment and even the desire to be punished for one's sins resurfaces again and again throughout this play. All the characters seem to view God as an unforgiving Judge of their lives, and they cannot forgive themselves unless some punishment cleanses them from their guilt. Having experienced earthly fathers whose lack of concern "punished" them with unhappy and impoverished childhoods, they seem to have but that one way of viewing their heavenly Father. Margaret cries, "Their death is my punishment. I am responsible for the death of my babies. I want to die" (56);

and her brother Billy tells Leonard after he murders Wally, "I wanted to be punished. I needed desperately to be punished" (97).

Mrs. Payne sums up this fixation on punishment when she cries to Leonard, "What's happening to us? The death of your two little boys. Wally's death. Your father's death. Have we committed some terrible sin? Are we being punished?" (99) Foote offers no insight into the cause of these tragedies; in most of his plays, he takes an attitude of acceptance, that these things happen in life and there is no answer, perhaps no reason, for them. He does not, however, support the conclusion that "punishment" is the final word. Just as often as one hears "punishment" in the play, one hears "forgiveness."

Uncle Virgil recalls a dream that offers insight into Foote's point: "I dreamt I was a boy still, eight or nine, and this Preacher was there and I was crying. He kept saying, 'Forgiveness,' and I kept crying and he kept saying, 'Forgiveness'" (129). That it is the Preacher in Virgil's dream who offers this word of wisdom and comfort may imply Foote's hidden message: the word of God is "forgiveness," not "punishment." One must not overlook, either, that both men in the play found guilty of murder are also given "suspended sentences." Though they are guilty, they are not required to "pay" for their crimes.

When Leonard later remembers his father's suicide note, he recalls, "It was something about debts and responsibilities and asking our forgiveness" (99). The role of the earthly father proved too much for Leonard's father, but because Leonard comes to realize he has failed his boys, too, he arrives at a compassionate understanding of his own father, too. He uses the memory of his father to help him cope with his own situation, as he tells his mother:

> I went out to the cemetery, to the little boys' graves, and I stood there between Papa's grave and their graves, and I went back over all that happened, and I tried to imagine what it would be like . . . for me now if Papa had never killed himself, or if I hadn't found his note and destroyed it; . . . But you know what I wanted most to change? Not that my little boys did not die. Not that. But that I would have the chance to love them again (99).

The use of the cemetery where connections are made and understandings are surmised is common to Foote's work but particularly significant in this piece. Recalling the role of one father, another father is able to come to terms with his own position. This matured insight into the necessity for mercy enables Leonard finally to forgive his wife.

While forgiveness may not lead to all the answers, it is the only path revealed for survival; maintaining ties with one's family, living and dead, may be the only road to salvation. "My family is here. My father is buried here, and my boys. My brother lives here . . ." (127), Leonard remembers, as he chooses to stay and work things out with his wife. In the final scene of the play, he confesses that although his heart is broken, he did it to himself; he has hope it will mend "in time" (130).

Leonard's ability to overcome his past and present traumas is credited to his eventual understanding of forgiveness. Billy, unfortunately, is unable to come to terms with his past or his present, allowing a poor relationship with his father as a child to poison his adult life, as well. He has never got over his father's affair with a young girl when he was a child; like his mother, he never spoke to his father again, eventually leaving Harrison to avoid contact with the man. Having first left town out of shame for his father, now he leaves again out of regret for something that his continued bitterness towards his father has driven him to do. Unable to forgive and forget, when he confronted Wally Smith, he confused the past with the present, his father with his sister. He tells Leonard: "I went to Wally Smith . . . [but] when I saw him, I started cursing him. For some reason I thought he was my father, and I cursed him; I called him all the filthy obscene names I had named my father all these years" (96).

Billy's resentment of his father has kept him locked in a prison of his own making all these years. Had he been able to express his hurt and shame to his father years ago, he might have purged his system; instead, by maintaining his resentful silence, the bitterness he felt toward the man festered into a poison that led to tragedy. Realizing this too late, he has lost all chance of true reconciliation. While Foote has been careful to sketch each character with a sense of charity and understanding, those characters who refuse to react similarly with one another cannot expect hopeful conclusions to their situations, and the pity one feels toward such characters is weighted with sadness for their chosen destinies.

Mrs. Payne, at one point in the play, muses that "there is a part of your life that belongs to the past, and as you grow older, the past becomes increasingly important to you" (13). The part fathers have played in the lives of their families and the influence they have been on their own children in the past certainly takes a very present role in the lives of these characters. Because Foote himself knows Mrs. Payne's observation to be true in his own life, he is able to write accurately about its truth in the lives of his characters. Dealing compassionately with each of his characters despite their mistakes in the play, Foote calls the audience to sympathize and understand these fictional representatives as fellow human beings.

That reconciliation and forgiveness, rather than resentment and punishment, are available is Foote's great theme in this final look at fathers and their children. The title of the play, taken from Isaiah 35:7, bears this out and strengthens the spiritual connections, as it speaks of hope. While the previous chapter of Isaiah may describe the impending judgement and destruction of the world, chapter 35 traditionally speaks of the peace of Christ's return. Verse seven, in its entirety, reads, "And the parched ground shall become a pool, and the thirsty land springs of water: in the habitation of dragons where each lay, shall be grass with reeds and rushes" (KJV). The chapter ends with verse ten: "And the ransomed of the Lord shall return, and come to Zion with songs and everlasting joy upon their heads: they shall obtain joy and gladness, and sorrow and sighing shall flee away." Foote may have taken the title out of context, but his message in the play is clear: though tragedy strikes, there is healing; though sins are committed, there is mercy; though earthly fathers are not all they should be for their children, the heavenly Father will not disappoint his children.

In a Coffin in Egypt (1980), the title also taken from a Bible verse, seems experimental for Foote.[8] While its stream-of-consciousness style has been championed by many of Foote's favorite writers, Faulkner and Katherine Anne Porter to mention only two, it is unique to Foote's work, which usually maintains a controlled dialogue. Set in the present, in the Texas town of Egypt, the play employs only two characters and no action whatsoever, as the 90-year-old Myrtle Bledsoe sits in her room, talking with her companion Jessie Lydell. Myrtle carries the bulk of the conversation, relying on free association to construct her story. One immediately is reminded of Katherine Anne Porter's "Jilting of Granny Weatherall," and it is no coincidence that Myrtle mentions Katherine Anne Porter as a great writer and the cousin of a friend in her monologues.[9]

Not only is Foote paying tribute to the author he considers one of his greatest influences (Personal Communication 11/14/87), he also is inviting the audience to make the connections between his character and Porter's. One recalls Porter's elderly lady thinking back over her life as she approaches death, allowing the memories of her rejection at the altar to swim into her monologue as they surface in her mind. This is exactly Foote's style as Myrtle chatters on and on about her past, revealing the bitterness she has felt toward her unfaithful husband Hunter all her life.

There is little of the father-child theme in *In a Coffin in Egypt*, but there is an understated note of the unconditional love between many fathers and their children, as Myrtle's daughters support their father, in spite of his multiple affairs during their childhood. Myrtle also recalls how her husband killed the father of the high school girl with whom he was having an affair when her father warned Hunter to stay away from his daughter. Myrtle's question to Hunter, "Does she love you now . . . that you've killed her Daddy?" puts her husband in his place. She describes the epitaph Iris had put on her father's tombstone: "Rest in Peace Daddy, Love, Iris" (40).

A father's influence on his children, for good or ill, is also referred to in several ways. First, when she wonders why her husband preferred black women over white for so many years, Myrtle remembers Hunter's father remarking that white boys "can have any Nigger on the place for twenty-five cents" (10).

The details of another local murder also weave their way into Myrtles reveries, as she tells of a twenty-year-old boy who shot his father. She blamed Hunter for giving the boy the idea when he killed his girlfriend's father: "He heard you saying, 'It was self-defense' . . . And he saw that you got off scott free" (32), she relates to Jessie, recalling how the boy echoed Hunter's words when he shot his father. Although Hunter was the boy's uncle and not his father, Myrtle sees him as the father-figure who, through his wanton living, gave the boy a bad example.

The impact of an unloving parent on a child, a point Foote's plays have supported before, is also brought out in a further observation Myrtle makes about the young murderer. She recalls hearing that the boy was convinced that his parents did not love him enough: "that's why he went off that way and did what he did" (45), she says. The idea that lack of parental love can lead to such insanity, violence, and grief is a strong statement, but not one Foote would hesitate making. In light of all the other examples of such problems resulting from poor parent-child relationships that have been discussed in Foote's other plays, it is unlikely that he is not making that point here.

From the first plays to the last, then, Foote has remained true to his created community, realistically but compassionately portraying their lives in all their joy and despair, boredom and excitement. In each, he has focused on the family as the nucleus of society, calling attention to its frayed edges and threadbare spots, as well as its strengths and beauty. The parent-child relationship has been highlighted, as the significance of the father-figure role shines through each family depicted. Not only has Foote recorded the lives and times of the types of people he knew, as he claims was his purpose in these writings, he has introduced the philosophy he holds for surviving these lives and times, and his vision, clear and straightforward, has not wavered. Though society as he sees it, depicted realistically in his plays, may have disintegrated, the old values of family, religion, and loving one's neighbor are still verities of life to be upheld and championed. This commitment distinguishes Foote's work from that of other

American playwrights and secures the author a unique place in modern theatre.

Notes

1 *The Man Who Climbed Pecan Trees* was produced first in 1982 at the Loft Studio of Los Angeles. It also was produced by the Ensemble Studio Theatre in 1988.

2 *The One-Armed Man* was produced in 1985 by HB Playwrights Foundations in New York City.

3 Directed by Calvin Skaggs, *The Roads to Home* was produced by the Manhattan Punch Line Theatre in New York City in 1982. It starred Hallie Foote in the role of Annie Gayle Long.

4 The HB Playwrights Foundation in New York produced *The Prisoner's Song* in 1985, along with *Blind Date* and *The One-Armed Man* under the collective title *Harrison, Texas*. Herbert Berghof directed.

5 *The Road to the Graveyard* opened in New York in 1985 at the Ensemble Studio Theatre.

6 Directed by Curt Dempster, *The Land of the Astronauts* was presented in New York in 1988 at the Ensemble Studio Theatre.

7 The first legitimate production of *The Habitation of Dragons* was at the Pittsburgh Public Theatre the fall of 1988, directed by Foote himself. Its workshop production in 1986 was in New York City.

8 *In a Coffin in Egypt* takes its title from the last phrase of the book of Genesis (50:26), which refers to the death and burial of Joseph. The allusion bears little significance to the interpretation of the play; it simply plays on the names of two locations, one in Africa and one in Texas, visited by the protagonist. She implies it makes little difference whether one is in Cairo, Egypt, or Egypt, Texas, as one ends up in a coffin somewhere.

9 *In a Coffin in Egypt* also is derivative of Tennessee Williams' *Glass Menagerie* (Foote's favorite Williams play), as it uses "rear projections" of the faces of the characters Myrtle discusses.

Chapter Seven

Horton Foote: An Assessment

"Stand-offish." "Close-mouthed." "Self-controlled." These are terms critics have used to describe Horton Foote's style of writing, whether they are applauding or dismissing his latest work.[1] Brooks Atkinson summed it up bluntly in a review for the New York *Times*: "He is the most tight-lipped playwright in the business" (CLC 130). For the most part, these reviewers are referring to Foote's quiet method of presenting low-key slices of small-town characters' lives in back-home Southern settings; others may refer also to Foote's reluctance to make caustic observations one way or the other explaining the situations he depicts. Atkinson adds, "Mr. Foote makes a moral point of never making a statement except in extremis" (130).

Samuel Freedman asserts that "Foote's determination to keep the emotional flame low . . . deeply divides critics and audiences" (xxiii). Many reviewers and movie-goers alike, preferring an outspoken or action-packed vehicle for entertainment, are impatient with such diffidence of style, as well as Foote's conservative content, and ignore or reject the "sepia-toned nostalgia . . . associate[d] with Foote" (Wallach, CLC 136). For this reason, perhaps, Foote's films have not been box-office hits, nor have many of his plays recently opened on Broadway. Those who appreciate Foote's quiet reminiscing refer to the same modest elements which have elicited these reviewers' negative response, however, and give Foote's work an equal body of rave reviews and create a growing following.

Vincent Canby of the New York *Times* defines Foote's style as one that "doesn't rush from one melodramatic incident to another" or "fret about keeping the audience's attention by artificial means." Acknowledging that this method will not appeal to everyone, he cautions, "to attempt to please everybody is to court the kind of madness that, in Hollywood, passes for sanity" (CLC 133). Calling attention to that "tight-lipped self-control" which may make it difficult initially to warm up to Foote's work, Canby urges the audience to be patient, as "the clarity and discipline of the writing" pay off richly in the end (CLC 132-133).

Foote justifies the "certain restraint [that] is part and parcel" of his style with, "It's just how I write." Realizing his form may not be commercial, Foote admits, "I'm not against jazzing things up, I just don't know anything about it!" He shrugs, "If that's your talent, that's your talent" (Sterritt 37). Canby again sums up what many critics have surmised by saying that this talent "represents the cinema of the playwright." He continues his praise with, "There is something revolutionary about a movie in which one has to pay attention to the dialogue and coordinate it with the images, which may or may not contradict what's being said" (New York *Times* 4/11/86:17).

"Revolutionary" indeed describes what Foote, tight-lipped or not, has accomplished in current film making. Edgerton sums up his assessment of Foote by suggesting, "Critical attention should increasingly focus on Horton Foote. . . . It is an exciting development to watch as more and more smaller-budgeted and localized film makers with the requisite talent and skills are now able to produce motion pictures with attitudes and styles that are unlike Hollywood formulas" (12), he concludes. David Sterritt offers even higher praise for Foote's mark on film making when he writes: "If anyone has a chance of reclaiming the word 'auteur' for authors—after years of seeing it used as a synonym for movie directors—it's certainly this soft-spoken Southerner, who's never afraid to reject the Hollywood rule book in favor of his own insights and instincts" ("Horton Foote" 1).

Foote's style of film making has been singled out and labeled as a "type," even by those who do not appreciate it. Freedman describes the "personal stamp" Foote's films bear: "In an age when the lexicon of cinema is largely visual," he writes, "Foote stresses dialogue and character development rather than spectacle or even traditional narrative." Foote finds Hollywood's enchantment with the visual at the expense of other film attributes "boring" (xxii-xxiii), ironically the same criticism given much of his work by those who desire Hollywood's stimulation.

While Foote's voice may be quiet, it has been heard loud and clear in his independent approach to making movies, especially by those who participate the most in film making, the actors. If Foote's is the "cinema of the playwright," as Canby claims, it is also the vehicle for the actor. Geraldine Page affirmed this assertion when she "blamed" Foote the night she won the Oscar for her portrayal of Mrs. Watts in *The Trip to Bountiful*. "It's all your fault, Horton," she teased, later admitting she had accepted the role sight-unseen, knowing that Foote "writes real characters using real dialogue" (Calio 75-76). In fact, the leading role in each of Foote's films nominated for Academy Awards has won the Best Actor/Actress Oscar every time; along with Page's *Trip to Bountiful*, Gregory Peck and Robert Duvall both won for *To Kill a Mockingbird* and *Tender Mercies*, respectively. While credit is due these respected actors, and to their directors, as well, surely acknowledgement is due the author who wrote their lines.

Although this study does not focus on performance, it would be remiss to overlook the importance of thoughtful acting in all films, Foote's particularly. Apparently, Foote's work has developed and maintained a respectable reputation with which actors have been unashamed, even eager, to associate themselves; Peck, Duvall, and Page mentioned above have accepted on more than one occasion roles in his films or plays, winning recognition beyond the Oscar for their portrayals of his characters. Foote claims Kim Stanley rose to stardom from her roles in his teleplays, and Matthew Broderick, a rising star of his own making, returns tirelessly to *The Orphans' Home* films, willingly giving his stamp of approval to this independent film maker's vision.

Critics of Foote's written work may be correct at times in complaining of his lackluster dialogue; on the page Foote's words can be prosaic at best. Foote defends his characters' conversation, insisting it is the realistic depiction of speech patterns of his small Southern community (Personal communication 11/13/87). He also goes on to prove incorrect Howard Hawks' assertion that "If it's wrong on the page, it'll be wrong on the big screen." Time and again careful actors breathe vibrancy into Foote's seemingly lifeless language, illustrating instead that "actors speak louder than words."

Again, these actors, who have brought accolades to Foote's material, rightly receive the praise for such effective expression, but Foote himself must share in the glory. Director Herbert Berghof credits Foote with the success: "The beauty of Horton Foote's work is that it is all his," he affirms. Robert Duvall, who cites Foote for "discovering" him and securing him his first film role as Boo Radley in *To Kill a Mockingbird*, agrees, "It's his writing. If he didn't write the way he does, I don't know if we'd be loyal" (Freedman xxiv-xxv). Soft-spoken as Foote may be, then, the actors involved in his works give a loud voice to his quiet, written words and call attention to the need for closer scrutiny of his work.

But film making is not the only medium in which Foote has sounded his low, yet unmistakable voice; the theatre, where his career began, echoes with Foote's tones. Although undeniably not the only playwright to dip into his personal past for literary material, Foote certainly may be the first to sustain one theme his entire career, as this study has revealed. His concentration on the family (personal and universal) is incessant throughout his canon from the first play to the last. And while other playwrights, Eugene O'Neill and Lanford Wilson particularly, have developed small collections of plays centering on one topic, Foote's *Orphans' Home* is the only cycle of its size to cultivate fully this one theme as reflected in the development of a single family.

John Simon, writing for *New York* Magazine, affirms this observation, even when his tongue is in his cheek:

> For many years now, Foote has been tirelessly churning out a continuous chronicle of his Texas family and their fellow small-towners. Written for stage, screen, and TV, these works could, laid end to end, outdistance Lanford Wilson's Talley plays ten times over, and may rival in length the family novels of Galsworthy, Romains, or Martin du Gard. . . . One must admire the mileage . . . Foote is able to get out of his simple ingredients (CLC 135).

Chilton Williamson, Jr., in *National Review* applies the point concerning Foote's cycle specifically to the entire Foote canon when he writes, "All [of Horton Foote's films] are, or seem to be, based on a cycle of stage plays . . . that form a family chronicle of his small-town Texas kinfolk" (CLC 135).

The creation of a cycle of work that maintains a single theme may be Foote's greatest contribution to American drama; Freedman confirms this view, stating, "The production and publication of the nine plays comprising the *Orphans' Home* cycle, Foote's family saga, guarantees him a deservedly permanent place in American letters" (xiii). Although this collection may be unique and worthy, still it is not Foote's only offering to our theatre. His steady adherence to the realistic depiction of a Southern community in all its minute detail serves not only as a record of the American past (and incidentally of Foote's own family, his primary purpose in writing), but also as a tribute to realism in the theatre. While other philosophies and methods in American drama have come and gone during Foote's lifetime, his steadfast grip on this approach to play writing has granted, at least in part, a permanence to the movement. A few other writers have stood just as firmly as Foote in upholding realism in the theatre, of course, but Foote's work stands as a monument to the cause. Evidence of Foote's role in maintaining American realism is manifested in his consistent, life-long preference to that approach. More important may be the development of his particular flavor of realism through his incessant focus on the small-town family; this focus gives his brand of realism, like his brand of film making, its own particular touch. It may be through his example that realism will continue to thrive in American drama.

It is his realistic depiction of the individual members of these small-town families that has instigated interest in his work and respect for his style. Critics and audiences alike, in a relatively small but growing number, confirm that they are drawn to Foote's plays and films because of a longing to see "real people, ordinary people" on the screen and stage again, rather than larger-than-life heroes or villains. Brooks Atkinson, as far back as 1954, cited this reason for his appreciation of Foote's plays: "In a theatre that is largely populated by decadent people who don't understand anything," he wrote, "it is a pleasure to watch Mr. Foote's characters behave like normal human beings" (CLC 130).

Foote has trusted his instincts which assure him that if he is interested in the minute details of "normal human beings," others are interested, too. Because he draws nearly all his characters from his personal family experience, he must assume that an audience also will find these relatives of his, as he depicts them, absorbing. Apparently this is a fair assumption. John Leonard, writing of *Story of a Marriage* for *New York* Magazine, attests, "For five and a half careful hours, the playwright Horton Foote remembers his own parents. I very much like his memories." Because Foote's characters are realistically portrayed, it is not hard to identify and sympathize with them. Leonard's appreciation of Foote's approach is affirmed by his belief in "every syllable of Horton Foote." He concludes, "He doesn't know how to lie" (CLC 138). Leonard's praise testifies particularly to the "Horton Foote Brand" of realism and his individual style of film making, made unique in a medium that relies on fantasy and the audience's suspension of belief.

Leonard goes on to call attention to another reason Foote's work has achieved popularity with its particular following: just as Foote has lent his quiet, but resounding voice to a specific kind of film and theatre, his script writing also has given a voice back to a group of mute American movie-goers who feel Hollywood no longer has anything to say to them or about them. The limited distribution of Foote's work, which makes it relatively unknown to mass America, may explain why this appreciative group is a "silent minority" rather than a majority.

Foote's aversion to coarse language and mature subject matter and his realistic depiction of morally-inclined characters is refreshing to those who have been offended by explicit sex, expletives, and excessive violence and whose only defense has been to stay away from the cinema and turn off the television. Leonard confesses, "*Story of a Marriage* is the only American mini-series this winter or spring that we can watch without feeling ashamed of ourselves" (CLC 138).

This appreciation of Foote's created milieu is more than just a moral issue; it is the longing for permanence in a too-quickly changing world that Foote's work embodies with which his audience also identifies. This reluctance to accept change "preoccupies" Foote's living and writing, as discussion of the works has mentioned, and perhaps his character Elizabeth sums it up best when she cries in *On Valentine's Day*, "I want everything to stay the way it is" (Freedman xvi-xvii). There is also a nostalgia which has swept forcefully through mid-America in the most recent decades, evident in everything from an obsession with old-time collectables and country-style decorating to a resurgence of the patriotism and conservative politics that were less conspicuous in the 1960's and 1970's. The more rapidly families break up or old buildings are torn down, for example, the more deeply Foote and his audience seem to long for unbreakable bonds and for things to remain the same.

Through his work, Foote seeks to crystallize a passing moment, his people and their heritage, and to pay them homage by eternizing their lives. The "biographical" purpose of Foote's writing is shared by the members of his audience who may turn to him in their inability to voice their reactionary longings, making his work as universal as it is personal. The scenes in his plays leaf by like pages in "a fondly regarded family album" (Wallach, CLC 136), and his films have the essence of what Richard Corliss of *Time* calls "a home-movie reverie . . . [a] convalescence from the electroshock therapy of current Hollywood film making" (CBY 147).

What Foote has to say is nothing new, unless, as the old song says, "Everything old is new again." And maybe that is the point Foote is trying to make in this revitalized stage of his career; his is a reminder to remember, to reclaim old values, to be reconciled to those with whom we may have lost touch. But Foote's voice is so soft, even when it is most insistent, that, as Leonard points out, "we have to slow down to hear him, and then what he says is not so much surprising as confirming: We knew that, didn't we?" (CLC 138).

For "confirming" is Foote's final word. "I guess I finally, deeply, inside myself do feel," Foote admits, "that in spite of all the chaos around us, there's an awful lot to celebrate in human beings" (Sterritt, "Human Being" 38). It is for this reason that he has focused on the family throughout his writing career. For although he has realistically depicted the family in all its broken imperfection (Freedman claims Foote "is no Norman Rockwell" [xviii]), Foote believes, as William Matthews wrote, "Family life is a disease for which family life is the only cure." No matter how fragmented the family Foote's work depicts, the plays rarely neglect suggesting the possibility for reunion between relatives.

That "the family institution [is] a potential source of personal stability" (CLC 128) is the message of Foote's work as this study's discussion of his emphasis on family has borne out. While he does not close his eyes to the reality of the family's disintegration, Foote does not turn his back on the possibility of reconciliation between family members. Not ignoring the disorder that Foote and his audience perceive in modern American society, Foote's examination of the confusion in the American family suggests his suspicion of the root of the problem.

Foote even goes so far in some of his works, such as *Tender Mercies* and *Trip to Bountiful*, to intimate that a deeper root to the problems which trouble both society and the family may lie in the broken spiritual relationships between human beings and God. Frank Rich, in the New York *Times*, suggests that Foote's characters are "searching for the spiritual sustenance of home" (CLC 136), as well as the physical or emotional nurturing they may hope to find there. Although Foote is careful to muffle this voice lest it cause any in his audience to turn a deaf ear, those who are listening cannot mistake its clear, though distant, tone.

It has been the purpose of this study to examine the role family plays in Foote's canon, highlighting the necessity of loving father-child relationships depicted in these works. Foote's careful characterization and his charity toward his characters also has been accentuated. The positive conclusions to these plays, in spite of the varied realistic situations portrayed, that Foote has maintained also has been illuminated, and the possibility of spiritual implications suggested by the material has been revealed. Finally, the establishment of Foote in the canon of modern American play writing has been supported.

In film making and in play writing, then, Foote's unique voice echoes, softly but surely, as his theme of family reconciliation exceeds his created or personal world to penetrate the living core of his audience. For although Foote himself may not need any more homecomings, there may still be a large number in his audience who appreciate a film or play that takes them back to the days when realistic, positive portraits of family-life were valued. And for those who share Foote's perspective and feel the need of his message in their own lives, on either the familial or spiritual level, Foote's invitation is encouraging: you *can* go home again. For as Calio writes in *People* Magazine, Foote *has* and has made a "beautiful career out of it, too" (76).

Notes

1 For a succinct study of Horton Foote's critical reviews from 1941-1987, see *Contemporary Literary Criticism*, 51: 128-138.

Works Cited

Barbera, Jack. "Tomorrow and Tomorrow and *Tomorrow*." *Southern Quarterly* (Spring/Summer) 1981.

Barnouw, Erik. *The Image Empire: A History of Broadcasting in the U.S.* Vol. III. New York: Oxford University Press, 1970.

Barr, George Terry. "The Ordinary World of Horton Foote." Unpublished dissertation. Knoxville, TN. 1986.

Burkhart, Marian. "Horton Foote's Many Roads Home: An American Playwright and his Characters." *Commonweal*. 26 February 1988: 110-115.

Calio, Jim and David Hutchings. "Drawing on his Clan's Past, Writer Horton Foote Unearths an Oscar-winning Bounty." *People Weekly*. 9 June 1986: 73-76.

Canby, Vincent. "Tomorrow." The New York *Times*. 10 April 1972, late ed.: 44:1.

———. "On Valentine's Day." The New York *Times*. 11 April 1986: 17.

Crowther, Bosley. "To Kill a Mockingbird." *The New York Times*. 15 Feb. 1963, late ed.: 10:2.

Edgerton, Gary. "A Visit to the Imaginary Landscape of Harrison, Texas: Sketching the Film Career of Horton Foote." *Literary/Film Quarterly*. January 1989.

Faulkner, William. "Address upon Receiving the Nobel Prize for Literature." In *The Portable Faulkner*. ed. Malcolm Cowley. New York: The Viking Press, 1974: 723-724.

―――. "Barn Burning." In *The Norton Anthology of American Literature*. Vol. 1, 2nd ed. eds. Nina Baym, *et al*. New York: W. W. Norton and Co., 1979: 492-1507.

―――. "Old Man." In *The Portable Faulkner*. ed. Malcolm Cowley. New York: The Viking Press, 1974: 481-581.

―――. "Tomorrow." In *Tomorrow and Tomorrow and Tomorrow*. eds. David G. Yellin and Marie Connors. Jackson: University Press of Mississippi, 1985: 33-52.

Foote, Hallie. Personal letter. Received 5 Sept. 1989.

Foote, Horton, screenwriter. *Baby the Rain Must Fall*. Dir. Robert Mulligan. Prod. Alan Pakula. With Steve McQueen and Lee Remick. Columbia, 1965.

―――, screenwriter. *Barn Burning*. American Short Story Series. PBS, 1980.

―――. *The Chase* [the play]. 1952. New York: Dramatists Play Service, 1980.

―――. *The Chase* [the novel]. New York: Rinehart, 1956.

――― and Lillian Hellman, screenwriters. *The Chase*. Dir. Arthur Penn. Prod. Sam Spiegel. Columbia, 1965.

―――. *Courtship, Valentine's Day, 1918: Three Plays from the Orphan's Home Cycle*. New York: Grove Press, 1987.

―――. *Courtship*. In *Story of a Marriage*. Dir. Howard Cummings. With Hallie Foote, William Converse-Roberts, and Amanda Plummer. PBS, 1987.

―――. *Cousins, The Death of Papa: Two Plays from The Orphan's Home Cycle*. NewYork: Grove Press, 1989.

―――, screenwriter. *The Displaced Person*. American Short Story Series. PBS, 1977.

——. "Flight." In *Television Plays for Writers: Eight Television Plays with Comment and Analysis by the Authors*. ed. Abraham Burack. Boston: The Writer, 1957.

——. *Harrison Texas: Eight Television Plays*. New York: Harcourt, Brace, 1956.

—— and Thomas Ryan, screenwriters. *Hurry Sundown*. Dir. and Prod. Otto Preminger. With Michael Caine and Jane Fonda. Paramount, 1966.

——. "In a Coffin in Egypt." Unpublished play. From Horton Foote's personal collection.

——. Interview. *The American Short Story*. With Calvin Skaggs, ed. New York: Dell, 1977.

——. Introduction. *Roots in a Parched Ground, Convicts, Lily Dale, The Widow Claire: Four Plays from The Orphans' Home Cycle*. By Horton Foote. New York: Grove Press, 1988.

——. "Ludie Brooks." Unpublished teleplay. Lamp Unto My Feet. NBC, 4 Feb. 1951. From Horton Foote's personal collection.

——, screenwriter. *1918*. Dir. Ken Harrison. Prod. Lillian Foote and Ross Milloy. With Hallie Foote, William Converse-Roberts, and Matthew Broderick. Cinecom International, 1985.

——. "Old Man." In *Three Plays*. New York: Harcourt, Brace, and World, 1962: 3-47.

——. "On First Dramatizing Faulkner." In *Faulkner, Modernism, and Film: Faulkner and Yoknapatawpha, 1978*. eds. Evans Harrington and Ann J. Abadie. Jackson: University Press of Mississippi, 1979: 49-65.

——. *Only the Heart*. New York: Dramatists Play Service, 1944.

———, screenwriter. *On Valentine's Day.* In *Story of a Marriage.* Dir. Ken Harrison. With Hallie Foote, William Converse-Roberts, and Matthew Broderick. PBS, 1987.

———. Personal communication. Louisville, KY: 13-15 November 1987.

———. Personal letter. Received 13 April 1987.

———. Personal letter. 21 December 1988.

———. Personal letter. 28 July 1989.

———. "The Rocking Chair." Unpublished teleplay. NBC, June, 1953. From Horton Foote's personal collection.

———. *Roots in a Parched Ground.* New York: Dramatists Play Service, 1962.

———. *Roots in a Parched Ground, Convicts, Lily Dale, The Widow Claire: The First Four Plays in The Orphans' Home Cycle.* New York: Grove Press, 1988.

———. *Selected One-Act Plays of Horton Foote.* ed. Gerald C. Wood. Dallas: Southern Methodist University Press, 1989.

———, screenwriter. *Story of a Marriage.* Dir. Howard Cummings. PBS, 1987.

———, screenwriter. *Tender Mercies.* Dir. Bruce Beresford. With Robert Duvall and Tess Harper. Universal, 1983.

———, screenwriter. *To Kill a Mockingbird* [the screenplay]. New York: Brentwood, 1964.

———. *Tomorrow.* Short story by William Faulkner. New York: Dramatists Play Service, 1963.

———. "Tomorrow." In *Tomorrow and Tomorrow and Tomorrow.* eds. David G. Yellin and Marie Connors. Jackson: University of Mississippi Press, 1985: 53-106.

——. *Tomorrow*. In *Tomorrow and Tomorrow and Tomorrow*. eds. David G. Yellin and Marie Connors. Jackson: University of Mississippi Press, 1985: 107-161.

——. "*Tomorrow*: The Genesis of a Screenplay." In *Faulkner, Modernism, and Film: Faulkner and Yoknapatawpha, 1978*. eds. Evans Harrington and Ann J. Abadie. Jackson: University of Mississippi Press, 1979: 149-162.

——. *The Traveling Lady*. New York: Dramatists Play Service, 1955.

——. "The Travellers." Unpublished teleplay. Goodyear Playhouse. NBC, 27 April 1952. From Horton Foote's personal collection.

——. *The Trip to Bountiful*. New York: Dramatists Play Service, 1982.

——, screenwriter. *The Trip to Bountiful*. Dir. Peter Masterson. Prod. Sterling van Wagenen and Horton Foote. With Geraldine Page, John Heard, and Rebecca de Morney. Film Dallas I and Bountiful Film Partners, 1985.

——. *A Young Lady of Property: Six Short Plays*. New York: Dramatists Play Service, 1983.

Forsberg, Myra. "Hallie Foote Relives Her Family's Past." The New York *Times* 13 April 1986, late ed.: 21-22.

Freedman, Samuel G. Introduction. *Cousins, The Death of Papa: Two Plays from The Orphans' Home Cycle*. New York: Grove Press, 1989.

Fristoe, Roger. Remarks. The Southern Baptist Theological Seminary FirstAnnual Conference on Religion and the Arts. Louisville, KY. 14 September 1989. [Referred to as SBTS].

Hachem, Samir. "Foote-Work." *Horizon*. April 1987: 39-41. "Horton Foote." *Current Biography Yearbook* 47 (1986): 143-147. [Referred to as CBY].

Hunter, Mary. Foreword. *Only the Heart*. By Horton Foote. New York: Dramatists Play Service, 1944. Kawin, Bruce. *Faulkner and Film*. New York: Frederick Unger Publishing Co., 1977.

Lee, Harper. *To Kill a Mockingbird*. New York: J. B. Lippincott Co., 1960.

———. "A Word." In *To Kill a Mockingbird*. Screenplay by Horton Foote. New York: Brentwood, 1964.

Locher, Frances Carol, ed. *Contemporary Authors*. Vol. 73-76, 1978.

McGrady, Mike. *Newsday II*. 22 December 1985: 7.

Millichap, Joseph R. "Horton Foote." *Dictionary of Literary Biography* 26 (1984): 101-104.

Neff, David. "Going Home to a Hidden God." *Christianity Today*. 14 April 1986: 30-31.

O'Connor, Flannery. "A Good Man is Hard to Find" and "The Displaced Person." In *The Complete Stories*. New York: Farrar, Straus, and Giroux, 1982.

Price, Reynolds. Introduction. *Courtship, Valentine's Day, 1918: Three Plays from The Orphans' Home Cycle*. By Horton Foote. New York: Grove Press, 1987.

Sargent, Alvin, screenwriter and Wendell Mayes, adaptor. *The Stalking Moon*. Dir. Robert Mulligan. Prod. Alan Pakula. With Gregory Peck and Eva Marie Saint. Warner Bros., 1968.

Skaggs, Merrill Maquire. "The Story and Film of *Barn Burning*." *Southern Quarterly* (Winter), 1983.

Sterritt, David. "Horton Foote: Filmmaking Radical With a Tender Touch." *The Christian Science Monitor*. 15 May 1986.

———. "Let's Hear it for the Human Being." *The Saturday Evening Post* (October), 1983: 36-38.

Wood, Gerald C. "Keynote Address." Southern Baptist Theological Seminary First Annual Conference on Religion and the Arts. Louisville, KY: 14 Sept. 1989. [Referred to as SBTS.]

———, ed. *Selected One-Act Plays of Horton Foote*. Dallas: Southern Methodist University Press, 1989.

———. and Terry Barr. "A Certain Kind of Writer." Interview with Horton Foote. *Literature/Film Quarterly*. 14:14 (1986). [Referred to as Wood, LFQ].

Young, Stark. Foreword. *The Traveling Lady*. New York: Dramatists Play Service, 1955.